PRAISE FOR *STORY OF OUR COUNTRY*

"A timely reminder of the diversity of the Labor tradition to help us consider and counter the challenges ahead."

JIM CHALMERS MP

"As Labor's primary vote in national elections drifts inexorably downwards, a fundamental debate about the party's purpose and beliefs is long overdue. *Story of Our Country* is a great place for that debate to commence. It is very refreshing that the debate about Labor's future will reflect Adrian Pabst's incisive, thoughtful, and well-researched argument about Labor's purpose and soul. It is particularly worthwhile that Pabst uses the lens of religious belief for the broad purpose of questioning the state of modern Labor's belief system, not to pursue a narrow religious agenda. In light of Chris Bowen's post-election observation that Labor had alienated many people of belief, it is a very timely perspective. Pabst concludes his analysis with some valuable insights that suggest a way forward, including a strong emphasis on the concept of vocation and a salient warning against the threat of 'meritocratic extremism'."

LINDSAY TANNER

"A timely reminder of a period when the Australian Labor Party was proud of, and benefited from, its Judeo-Christian heritage and respect for faith-based conservative traditions. And a guide to how Labor might revitalise itself after the 2019 election defeat."

GERARD HENDERSON

THE KAPUNDA PRESS

Series editor: *Damien Freeman*

Fellow of the PM Glynn Institute, Australian Catholic University

The Kapunda Press is an imprint of Connor Court Publishing
in association with the PM Glynn Institute

CHALICE OF LIBERTY

PROTECTING RELIGIOUS FREEDOM IN AUSTRALIA

Frank Brennan – M. A. Casey – Greg Craven

(2018)

TODAY'S TYRANTS

RESPONDING TO DYSON HEYDON

Frank Brennan – Anne Henderson – Paul Kelly – M. A. Casey – Peter Kurti
M. J. Crennan Hayden Ramsay – Shireen Morris – Michael Ondaatje
Sandra Lynch – Catherine Renshaw

(2018)

FEDERATION'S MAN OF LETTERS

PATRICK MCMAHON GLYNN

Anne Henderson – John Fahey – Anne Twomey – Peter Boyce
Suzanne Rutland – Patrick Mullins

(2019)

Forthcoming:

NONSENSE ON STILTS

RESCUING HUMAN RIGHTS IN AUSTRALIA

M. A. Casey – Damien Freeman – Catherine Renshaw – Bryan S. Turner
Emma Dawson – Nicholas Aroney – Jennifer Cook – Terri Butler – Tim Wilson

(2019)

THE MARKET'S MORALS

RESPONDING TO JESSE NORMAN

Tania Aspland – Gregory Melleuish – Amanda Walsh – Adrian Pabst
Michael Easson – Parnell McGuinness – David Corbett – Cris Abbu – Tom Switzer
Marc Stears – Leanne Smith – M. A. Casey

(2019)

Story of Our Country

Labor's vision for Australia

Adrian Pabst

Published by Connor Court Publishing under the imprint of The Kapunda Press. The Kapunda Press is an imprint Connor Court Publishing in association with the PM Glynn Institute, Australian Catholic University.

CONNOR COURT PUBLISHING PTY LTD
PO Box 7257
Redland Bay QLD 4165
online@connorcourt.com
www.connorcourtpublishing.com.au

ISBN: 978-1-926826-59-3 (pbk.)

Cover design by Ian James

Cover picture: Mervyn Napier Waller, mosaic in dome of the Hall of Memory (1952-58), Australian War Memorial reference number PAIU2002/165.11

Printed in Australia

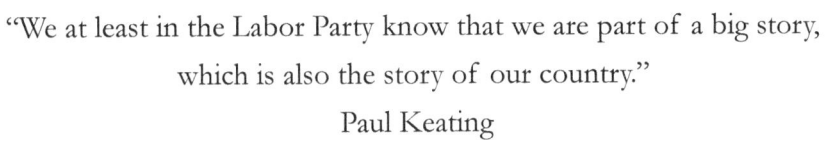

"We at least in the Labor Party know that we are part of a big story,
which is also the story of our country."
Paul Keating

Contents

Acknowledgements

The idea for this book emerged in conversations with Damien Freeman in Cambridge during the summer of 2017. At a time when centre-left parties across the West were losing elections and staring at the prospect of years in the political wilderness, Australian Labor seemed to be on course for office. Losing the 2019 federal election raises questions about the party's purpose and character, which this work explores. The ALP has not won a majority since 2007 and it struggles to build coalitions between its traditional working-class base and middle-class voters. The focus of the book is on ideas of justice and democracy anchored in the everyday existence of people, which Labor needs to renew in order to gain and retain power.

In 2018, while on Study Leave, I had the honour of being appointed to a visiting fellowship by the PM Glynn Institute, the Australian Catholic University's public policy think-tank, for which I am especially grateful to the director, Dr Michael Casey, as well as to the vice-chancellor, Professor Greg Craven AO GCSG and the pro-chancellor, Julien O'Connell AM. It has been an immense pleasure to work with them and with other colleagues at ACU, and I would also like to thank Samantha Dunnicliff of the PM Glynn Institute for her assistance.

My visiting fellowship was named for Sir Peter Lawler OBE GCPO who was responsible for drafting the Cabinet paper that led to the abolition of the White Australia Policy and one of the first Catholics appointed to head a Commonwealth government department in the post-war era. Sir Peter's outstanding example of public service is illustrated by the way he seamlessly combined being a life-long supporter for the ALP with being a trusted servant of governments of different political persuasions. My thanks go to his daughter Geraldine and her husband Phil for sharing with me a copy of Sir Peter's memoirs and memories of his extraordinary life.

During two stays in Australia in 2018, I had the great fortune of meeting with ALP parliamentarians, in particular the Hon. Linda Burney MP, Dr Jim Chalmers MP, Senator the Hon. Jacinta Collins, Senator Patrick Dodson, Chris Hayes MP, the Hon. Dr Andrew Leigh MP, Senator Jenny McAllister, Senator the Hon. Kristina Keneally, Matt Keogh MP, Madeleine King MP, Senator Deborah O'Neill, and the Hon. Wayne Swan MP. I owe each of them a debt of gratitude for their time and generosity.

I also learned much from conversations with Tom Bentley, Professor Frank Bongiorno, Frank Brennan SJ AO, Joe de Bruyn, Michael Costigan, Gerard Dwyer, Stephen Elder, Professor James Franklin, Danny Gilbert AM, Dr Rosie Hancock, Kate Harrison Brennan, Anne Henderson AM and Dr Gerard Henderson, Race Mathews, John McCarthy QC KCSG, Professor Greg Patmore,

Charles Power, Chris Sidoti, Professor Marc Stears, Professor John Warhurst, Andrew West, and Dr Nigel Zimmermann.

My enduring thanks go to Dr Michael Easson AM for conversations about the influence of Burkean on the ALP, and to Dr Nick Dyrenfurth for sharing ideas and material with me. Both Michael and Nick did me the honour of commenting on the manuscript, and their suggestions were invaluable. Michael Cooney, Damian Grace, and Eric Sheng also offered comments on my text. I am particularly indebted to Damien Freeman, now principal adviser to the director of the PM Glynn Institute, who was a constant source of advice on all aspects of the work.

Finally, I am grateful for the support and friendship of Professor Wayne Hudson, Professor Greg Melleuish, and Dr John Rees in Australia, as well Jason Cowley, Dr Jon Cruddas MP, Lord Glasman, Professor John Milbank, Dr James Noyes, and Professor Jonathan Rutherford in Britain.

The book would not have been possible without the loving patience of my family.

Adrian Pabst, London, 9 July 2019

Introduction

The power of purpose

Story of our country

Muhammad Ali once said that "you never get knocked out by a punch you see coming". It is a good rule in politics, too. After three years of being ahead in the opinion polls, the Australian Labor Party (ALP) lost the 2019 federal election that had been billed as 'unlosable'. Much like the British Labour Party in Britain's 2015 general election that lost to the Conservatives, the ALP looked set to win but suffered a crushing, albeit narrow, defeat at the hands of the Coalition. It is one of the most spectacular results in Australia's political history, which few predicted and hardly anybody in Labor expected. The ALP failed to secure the popular vote for the third election in a row. It did not convince two-thirds of Australians, notably those who live in suburbs and rural regions, and no opposition wins without earning the people's trust. A majority of Australians are not primarily interested in policies or political personalities, but in the broadest sense care about family, friends, work, community, and country. Labor's raft of policy ideas failed to convey a commitment to these fundamental values. Fighting climate change and closing tax loopholes are important yet secondary concerns. The primary priorities are secure, meaningful jobs to feed one's family and a sense of belonging to both people and place.

To gain power and govern in the national interest, the ALP has to reform its party organisation, political culture, and policy agenda, which are underpinned by a working philosophy. What is the party's purpose? Who does it represent? How does it protect the people it was set up to speak for? If defending the labour interest and working people are the answer, then the wider question is about the party's ethical outlook. What are the principles anchored in the values and beliefs of the labour movement that animate the ALP? How do the party's organising principles shape its political and policy platform? Since its inception in the 1890s, the ALP's moral purpose has been closely connected to the 'fair go' – justice for all and the protection of the 'Australian way of life'. Much like 'mateship', the fair go is a contested notion that evolved over time and is invoked by politicians across the political spectrum. By laying claim as the only party of the fair go, the ALP at its best seeks to represent more than class, ideology or sectional interest. Its ambition is to be a party of the people and the nation. In the words of Paul Keating, "We at least in the Labor Party know that we are part of a big story, which is also the story of our country".[1]

From the outset, the ALP's purpose was to link the representation of the labour interest in national politics to a wider aspiration: enabling people to pursue the good life. After the 1890 Maritime Strike, the party's founders declared that only by securing representation in the federal parliament "can we . . .

ensure to every man, by the opportunity of fairly remunerated labour, a share in those things that make life worth living".[2] Labor considers rewarding work as a contribution to shared prosperity that is at the heart of a secure and meaningful life. This is one of its most enduring principles, which draws sustenance from the labour movement and kindred national traditions, including the social justice tradition of the churches – a key focus to which I shall return throughout this book. The emphasis on rewarding work, which provides not just an income but also a sense of self-worth and meaning, is an example of how economic and socio-cultural concerns overlap and converge with ethical considerations. Linking them together is a certain conception of justice centred on the common good, which can be defined as an ordering of relationships in a way that holds in balance individual fulfilment with mutual flourishing, based on the dignity and equality of all people.

Politics of the common good

The common good transcends the small-l liberal accentuation of individual rights and the utilitarian emphasis on private or public happiness. It is bound up with the practice of virtue – a habit or quality that enables human beings to pursue the goals that are internal to activities, like being a good mother, neighbour, friend, colleague or fellow citizen. An understanding of justice based on virtuous behaviour and the common good helps to discourage the vices of greed, selfishness, distrust, and conflict in favour of common benefit, generosity, trust, and cooperation on which both a functioning democracy and market economy depend. Otherwise, the Labor-inspired post-war reconstruction model of socially embedded markets, a balance of open economies with protection of domestic employment and industry, and a commitment to the dignity of the person embodied in human rights risks becoming debased. It slides, as has happened over the past twenty years or so, into cartel capitalism, bureaucratic overreach, unfettered globalisation, and rampant individualism.

When, in the late nineteenth century, liberal democracies experienced the demoralising and dehumanising consequences of untrammelled capitalism, mass factory production, 'freedom of contract' to the employer to arbitrarily hire and fire, together with radical, contesting forces, it was the emergence of both the labour movement and Catholic social teaching (starting with Pope Leo XIII's social encyclical *Rerum Novarum* in 1891) that offered a constructive alternative to liberal individualism without falling into statist collectivism – the totalitarian state of fascist and Communist regimes. This new alternative based on intermediary institutions and working-class self-organisation was instrumental in enshrining into Western politics notions of solidarity, subsidiarity, and the common good. Solidarity means lived fraternity between people. Subsidiarity denotes the devolution of power to the lowest level in line with dignity, so that people may flourish and partake of the public good – beginning with secure, meaningful work and safe neighbourhoods.

A politics of the common good starts from where people are and reflects what they value. Australians share a love of the land, an attachment to work and to the family, affection for mates, scepticism about authority, and opposition to privilege. In his 2016 book, *For the Common Good*, the former Labor leader Bill Shorten described the common good as the attempt to

> bring together the people of this country—the men, women,
> children and families of our inner cities, suburbs, regions and
> remote communities; Indigenous, local and immigrant; small and
> big business, workers and unions; young and old; progressive and
> conservative. It's time to move past the cycle of division that has
> characterised our politics for too long. At Federation in 1901,
> Australians consciously chose to unite under the name of the
> 'Commonwealth of Australia'. Our nation was born in a spirit of
> shared purpose, mutual respect and equal sacrifice. In 2016, we
> Australians must rediscover our ability to work together for the
> common good.[3]

The situation in 2019 is fundamentally unchanged. At a time when economic inequality is increasing, politics polarised, and society fragmented, Labor needs to build bridges and offer a majority politics. But economic globalisation, combined with a decline in union density and technological disruption, has eroded the ALP's working-class base of industrial blue-collar and white-collar workers living precarious lives. They are no longer Labor's core electorate. This is because the party appears to embrace an aggressively secular, liberal ideology that blithely and complacently equates all change with progress. In reality, what is gained can just as easily be lost. A of lot of change does not benefit the working class, especially where 'progress' leads to economic and cultural insecurity. Many see the ALP as indifferent to their plight. For that reason, Labor needs to reconcile estranged interests in the direction of shared prosperity and social cohesion. This requires a break with the individualism of the Liberal Party and the statism of the traditional Labor Left in favour of a sense of reciprocity and mutual obligations.

Labor's Christian-inspired ethos

Labor history is replete with this ethos, notably Irish and Italian working-class Catholics, middle-class Anglicans, and Nonconformists, such as the Presbyterian Labor Prime Minister Andrew Fisher and the Methodist lay preacher William Guthrie Spence, co-founder of the Australian Workers' Union and early Labor MP.[4] Most ALP leaders and prime ministers were either Christians – such as Jim Scullin, Ben Chifley, Paul Keating, and Kevin Rudd – or shaped by Christianity – including John Curtin, Gough Whitlam, Bob Hawke, and Julia Gillard. The latter may have lost their faith but they remained broadly committed to Christian ethics.[5] Recent instances of Christian influence on Labor politics include Shorten's book on the common good and Anthony Albanese's statement that "Mum raised me with three great faiths: the Catholic Church, the South Sydney football club and Labor. She said to be true to all three. Well, with regard to the Catholic Church, I believe that the social justice values that I was raised with, I have kept".[6] These are but a few examples of the residual, albeit continual, presence of Christian ideas in the ALP. Those ideas resonate with other founding traditions, such as the trade union movement, partly because of their common roots in Australia's Christian heritage and partly because of a shared belief in social justice. The importance for today and going forward is that Labor only wins and governs in the national interest when it is a broad church that holds different traditions in balance.

Such has been the impact of the Royal Commission into sexual abuse, however, that few now look to the churches as a moral compass in politics. All of them, in particular the Roman Catholic Church, are to some degree discredited and so too, sadly, is much of the good work they do across society – especially in health and education. This is surely a cultural, moral, and societal loss to the nation. Without trust in the church and its institutions, appeals to the social justice tradition ring faintly. The bells of old go untolled or unheard. What the abuse scandal reveals is not just the depravity of individual priests and many instances of institutional cover-up, but also a deep-seated moral corruption combined with a lack of leadership. This is further handicapped by the perceived arrogance of parts of the church hierarchy. While more robust mechanisms are in place to avoid more abuse cases, the hierarchy must do much better at acknowledging past crimes and addressing the damage done to victims. In addition and connected with this, there is generally a greater mistrust of institutions in light of revelations by royal commissions into financial misconduct, age-care facilities, and trade unions, and of political organisations, as witnessed by low party membership and growing disaffection from parties. The institutions which were indicative of the strength of our society are weak, disrespected and, in some cases, broken.

In this context, the social justice tradition of the churches can make an important contribution by recognising the reality of vice and sinfulness, including within the churches, while at the same time charting a path that avoids empty moralism in favour of transformative action. Indeed, Catholic social teaching and comparable traditions in other Christian denominations promote 'principled practices', which is to say educational, charitable, civic, and economic activities that demonstrate to people how the gospel can transform their lives in reality. In this manner, Christian social teaching offers a rich sense of justice and healing. In our time, this – combined with, say, Pope Francis's moral authority – can provide the leadership necessary to promote the public good. It is a noble ambition shared with the ALP, the one party in Australia shaped by both the wider labour movement and the social justice tradition of the churches. The presence of Catholic social teaching in the Labor Party is implicit, tacit, and assumed, and also incremental, iterative, and intuitive. In this sense, it is not a matter of doctrine but rather a proximate influence – a certain disposition towards justice and the good life rather than a fixed ideological position. How the commitment to the common good translates into the ALP's political platform and its policy ideas is the subject of this book.

Chapter 1 focuses on the party's present predicament and the reasons for its three consecutive defeats (2013, 2016, and 2019), but also the potential to offer a majority politics that is lacking from other centre-left parties in the Western world. The ALP can achieve this by once again being true to both its radical and its small-c conservative character. Chapter 2 turns to the past and shows that the influence of Burkean ideas and Christian social teaching varied significantly over time but was almost always a strong undercurrent that shaped the party – even after the 1955 split with the break-away Democratic Labor Party (DLP) and growing divides along religious-ideological lines pitting progressives against conservatives.

In Chapter 3, the focus shifts to the deep philosophical beliefs and traditions that underpin the Australian labour movement. While egalitarianism and small-l liberalism have been present in the ALP for much of its history, Burkean ideas and Catholic personalism are just as important to understand the party's ethical outlook – a commitment to economic justice and social stability that creates the conditions for people to pursue a good life. Chapter 4 explores how the philosophical framework shapes the political platform and policy agenda. The ALP at its best seeks to defend the dignity of work and workers, promote democracy in the workplace, foster shared prosperity, build a safety net for those who cannot help themselves, and provide public investment in health, housing, education, and transport, as well as assuring Australians that it will keep them safe. These political goals and policy positions are underpinned by a deeper vision of the good society that offers Australians the opportunity to enjoy stable and meaningful lives. Of course, the ALP is not free from factionalism, ideological division, personal ambition, and vested interests, but the promise of a "share in those things that make life worth living" means that we can hold the ALP to a far higher standard than mere party unity or expedient pragmatism. The reason is that Labor's rich history of ideas and reforms draws on Burkean thinking and the social justice tradition of the churches.

Why Catholic social teaching?

It might be queried why the particular emphasis in this book is on Catholic social thinking, and whether there is anything exclusive or in contest with other denominations in this characterisation. One simple explanation is that the written evidence of Catholic engagement with the Australian labour movement is more evidence-rich than for other churches, particularly since the late nineteenth century when papal encyclicals and Catholic polemics discussed the way that religious lay-persons should interpret and engage with the world around them. Other faiths, including the Jewish and Muslim traditions of *tikkun olam* in Hebrew, *islah* in Arabic, also emphasise the obligation to act constructively and beneficially in society, and to offer succour to those most in need. In both the Qur'an and Talmud, it is said that if a person saves one life, it is as though they have saved all of humanity. Many of the ideas in this book can easily apply to other faiths, also neglected by the ALP in its contemporary engagement with Australian society.

Historically, the Christian churches and individual Christians were incredibly important to the early labour movement, the formation of the ALP, and in the development of that party until comparatively recent times. Outside of the Catholics, who particularly became influential after the splits in the ALP in 1916-17 over conscription, some of the other Christian churches eschewed active engagement with the labour movement, preferring aloofness. One account of the Anglican tradition in Australia notes that: "The reluctance of dominant elements within the church to encourage a national identity had implications for relationships with the working class...",[7] particularly as the fledgling labour movement became associated with Australian nationalism. Alas, "Anglican bishops believed that they should stand above party politics and, unlike their Roman Catholic fellows, established no formal links with Labor".[8] Lance Shilton, the then Dean of St Andrew's Cathedral in Sydney, in a publication on the fiftieth anniversary of the formation of the Australian Council of Trade Unions (ACTU) wrote:

> Let us now be quite frank. Churchmen for the most part have neglected their responsibilities within the labour movement... The Roman Catholics have maintained an interest – politically motivated, but in recent years that too has become less influential. With more friendly relationships between Christian denominations there are now new opportunities for co-operative effort in making the much needed spiritual impact.[9]

Apart from some joint statements in the 1980s on common concerns, particularly concerning the 'permissive society', there is not much evidence of the co-operation between churches that Dean Shilton hoped for.

In a major recent study on evangelical Christianity in Australia to 1914, the authors highlight the substantial involvement of adherents to the Methodist, Presbyterian, and other Non-Conformist churches in the early days of union organisation and in the formation of the ALP. The first wave of Labor MPs were mostly Protestants. Individuals of that persuasion were always important in the party. But neglect by the leading Protestant clergymen meant more space for Catholics with their engagement with the party. The authors of the study remark, as one example: "The failure of the Methodists to evolve a strongly-based Christian philosophy of social action on behalf of working men was a tragedy".[10] Whatever the reasons for neglect on all sides, the issue today is to recover old links and to seek renewed inspiration.

Indeed, in the past these traditions were prominent within the ALP, in particular for those of Catholic working-class heritage which was not confined to Irish immigrants but extended to the many other Europeans who came to shape the nascent nation of modern Australia.[11] Crucially, the Labor party was a place of reconciliation between Catholics, Anglicans, Evangelicals, and Nonconformists around notions of justice and the dignity of work. The appeal of Christian social teaching was its attempt to reject both the rampant individualism associated with laissez-faire capitalism and the collectivism associated with totalitarian communist ideology in favour of a socially embedded market and a plural state, which can promote the common good, as I have already indicated.

Based on the principles of Catholic social thought, Catholic thinkers, such as G. K. Chesterton and Hilaire Belloc, developed the idea of distributism, which refers to the distribution of productive assets among the people for the purpose of their greater autonomy from both centralised bureaucracy and big business. In accordance with the principle of subsidiarity, distributism favours workplace democracy and mutual models of enterprise, which translates into a policy agenda of spreading private ownership of housing and democratic control of industry through owner-operated businesses and worker-controlled cooperatives. These ideas shaped the Australian labour movement, especially in Victoria where the ALP promoted Catholic principles of social justice that resonated strongly with local independent communities, as Race Mathews has shown.[12] In addition, many moderate socialists (often described as guild socialists), who emphasise the primacy of worker associations over the central state, drew on Christian ethics in order to promote alternatives to laissez-faire liberal capitalism and statist socialism or communism. These alternatives influenced Labor right up to the adoption of the 'socialisation' pledge in 1921 by the national ALP conference.[13] Labor's legacy of searching for constructive settlements is a rich source for political and policy ideas today.

Why Burkean ideas?

Story of Our Country explains how the traditions of Burkean thinking, Christian and Catholic social thought formed part of the ALP's original ethical outlook and can once more be resources for Labor policy-making. My reference to Burke, who is so often narrowly misconstrued as a mere conservative, and to Christian traditions, might seem eccentric in reference to a party that now appears to be deeply progressive and secular. As might seem my characterisation of small-c conservative and Burkean instincts as useful searchlights for appreciating Australian Labor's ethos. My points only appear contradictory to those who think in a linear or one-dimensional way – and to those without appreciation for the ALP's history. Each of us are combinations of complex belief systems, feelings, instincts, and behaviours. Characteristics like loyalty, solidarity, respect for the ethos of a movement, as well as an active understanding of the traditions of a political party, particularly the ALP, are at once radical and conservative, inspiring reference points to an on-going journey. Historically, labourist, socialist, liberal, and conservative tendencies are in unique combination part of the ferment of Australian Labor, a political movement motivated by moral purpose. Australian Labor can deploy its deep appreciation for the complexities of political and economic choices, the paradoxical characteristics of political solutions, by better understanding where it has come from. I say that timeless principles inspired by the churches are a guide and means in our time for the ALP to better connect with and govern for the Australian people.

What is the significance of Burkean ideas and Christian social thinking for Labor today? The idea of an alternative to both libertarian individualism and authoritarian collective control associated with state capitalism could hardly be more significant. At a time when the consensus on market liberalism and social progressivism is in question, *Story of Our Country* explores how the traditions of Burkean ideas, Catholic social teaching, and distributism offer both a narrative and a set of policy ideas, which can help the ALP not just to gain and retain power but also govern in the national interest. Burkean ideas of a civic covenant between the generations and social Catholicism can marry economic interests with cultural concerns, especially among working-class voters who traditionally were among the party's bedrock electoral support. Arguably, Labor needs to do much better at building a strong, broad cross-class and cross-cultural coalition. It cannot win without its traditional supporters who are more socially conservative than the progressive urban middle class. As Barry Jones – a minister in the Hawke Government and former ALP President – suggested in 2004:

> The ALP is not, and should not be, simply a machine that organises election campaigns every few years – it needs to provide spiritual, ethical and intellectual nourishment to the Australian people, and promote a creative, generous nation. At present, there is a significant disenfranchisement of our traditional vote, people who feel lonely and alienated from the Party they have always voted for. If we do not bring them home, the Party's heart and mind will die.[14]

Labor's purpose

In our age of polarised politics and mutual demonisation, many will be understandably sceptical about any talk of moral purpose. How else to offer "spiritual, ethical and intellectual nourishment" other than by way of vision? Surely the Old Testament wisdom is right that "where there is no vision, the people perish".[15] The ALP's animating energy has always been expressed in the power of words – from William Spence's "unionism is merely the teaching of He of Nazareth" and John Curtin's "the compass of the labour movement" to Ben Chifley's "Light on the Hill" and "things worth fighting for", Gough Whitlam's "I put into your hands this piece of earth itself", Bob Hawke's "the spirit of men and women yearning to be free", Joan Child's "Parliament was the instrument of our cause", Paul Keating's Redfern Speech, his post-election speech "for the true believers", his eulogy "he is all of them and he is one of us", and Kim Beazley's "There are dark angels in our nation but there are also good angels". And recently Kevin Rudd's "we are sorry", Julia Gillard's "I will not", and Bill Shorten's "If you think that Labor is too weak, bring it on". Woven into the tapestry of Australian history and pregnant with religious imagery, these speeches reflect the "story of our country".

The Labor Party tends to win elections and become the dominant force in Australian politics when it tells a credible story about national renewal – giving people reason to hope for a better future. Politics and policy require a clear sense of purpose that transcends power and wealth in the direction of mutual recognition, reciprocity, and the joint quest for the common good. Hard work, family, community, and country are things valued by a majority in Australia. The challenge for Labor is balancing them with its progressive principles of equality, diversity, and redistributive justice. Without succeeding in this balancing act, Labor will struggle to recover its appeal among its traditional electoral base. The party and the wider labour movement need to be with the people and embody Labor's original purpose: offering everyone a share of the good life.

1

Present
The ALP's positioning

Labor's 'progressive dilemma'

Labor's defeat in the 2019 federal election was unexpected though not surprising. Weaknesses were masked. The ALP had been ahead in the polls for three years after nearly winning the 2016 contest. Promisingly for Labor, the governing Coalition was divided and directionless during the years of Malcolm Turnbull's premiership. If the old adage holds true that "oppositions do not win elections, governments lose them", then Labor looked set for victory. The ALP leadership never anticipated losing any seats to the Liberals. But Scott Morrison ran a presidential leader's campaign that exposed Bill Shorten's lack of popularity – a decent man who could not connect enough with the party's previous working-class base of blue-collar and white-collar workers living precarious lives. Labor did well enough among urban middle-class professionals but lacked support from its traditional base in Australia's suburbs and rural regions. Like other social-democratic sister parties, the ALP did not manage to build alliances across social, cultural, and geographic boundaries in search of majority support.

The English academic and former British Labour MP David Marquand conceptualised this tension within the centre-left as the 'progressive dilemma' – the clash between working-class demands for radical economic change and a middle-class preference for cautious reform.[1] This tension characterises all social democratic parties. Potentially Labor's loss reflects social democracy's decline and slide into minority politics. I say 'potentially' because the verdict lies ahead. A courageous confronting of the reasons for the 2019 election debacle is needed. It would be a mistake to think a particular policy alone was the problem. There is an attitude or disposition issue. And that goes to the heart of how Labor is perceived. The ALP's election platform spoke to the problem of low wage growth but failed to address the wider economic insecurity of the less affluent middle class as well as the new working class in the service economy. Above all, the party did not respond sympathetically to the deeper anxiety of both industrial and regional workers about the lack of secure, meaningful jobs. As the chapter argues, the ALP put doctrine before politics and did not reflect the party's best traditions of fusing a radical with a small-c conservative disposition reflecting a majority concern for economic justice and social cohesion.

The ALP's defeat was unsurprising because of the party's failure to carry what were its core voters. This has been decades in the making. Labor's primary vote first fell below 40 percent in the 1990 elections and never really recovered. The exception was 1993 – a shock victory that few predicted and hardly anyone outside of die-hard Keating supporters expected. In 2019, the Liberals did to Labor what Labor did to them in 1993. Apart from a comfortable victory in 2007 that would evaporate less than three years later, the long-term trend has been downward. From 2010 to 2019, the ALP's popular vote was in the 30s. In three consecutive elections Labor failed to take enough seats from the Liberals outside metropolitan middle-class areas. In 2019, the Coalition held virtually all the marginal seats and won seats from the ALP in Tasmania and New South Wales. Neither Western Australia nor South Australia delivered any seats that Labor needed to win. But it was in Queensland where the 2019 contest was ultimately lost. The primary popular vote for the ALP was a paltry 26 percent, and the swing to the Liberals ended Labor's hope of becoming the largest party in Parliament and forming government. Only one Senate seat (out of six) in Queensland was won by the ALP. In his first speech to the party caucus following the election, the new Labor leader, Anthony Albanese, acknowledged as much when he said "we received the support of one in three Australians, as their first preference. In Queensland, that figure was one in four".[2]

There was nothing inevitable, however, about the ALP's defeat. On the contrary, the party seemed to recover from the 2013 federal elections when its primary vote dipped below 34 percent for the first time in 80 years with a loss of 17 seats. In the space of just six years, Labor had gone from a landslide victory in 2007 to a rout in 2013. After half a decade of division between Kevin Rudd and Julia Gillard, the ALP faced the prospect of years in the political wilderness.[3] The party's identity as a national popular force in Australian politics was at stake, including its hard-fought reputation for reforming the country in times of economic turmoil. This was done successfully in the 1980s and following the 2008 global financial crisis. Under Bill Shorten's leadership, the 2016 election saw Labor reduce the parliamentary majority of the governing Liberal Party to a single seat. At the time of writing, the ALP holds government in three out of the six states, as well as the two territories. While Shorten's rating as potential prime minister always lagged behind those of the various Liberal leaders, federal Labor held a consistent election-winning lead and looked poised for government.

In the past, Paul Keating used to describe Liberal Party leaders from Robert Menzies to John Howard as being "asleep at the wheel", on automatic, but directionless. This applied to the premiership of Malcolm Turnbull, when the Coalition was riven by ideological and personality battles. By contrast, the Labor Party united in opposition and progressively sharpened its focus on inequality, especially in an economy where the Australian promise of a 'fair go' is no longer realised in practice. The ALP's case for a more ethical economy – raising real wages, clamping down on financial misconduct, boosting investment in education, health and housing – was proving principled and seemingly popular. The political chaos within the government made victory there look for the plucking. The ALP had unity, a functioning front bench with lots of women active in the campaign, and policies as far as the eye could see.

Labor, however, lacked an overarching narrative capable of winning back its working-class base while also convincing the middle class. On one level their interests might diverge, as the former face an economic situation characterised by stagnant wages, low household savings, and insecure work, whereas the latter confront a ceiling on their aspiration which is linked to the hollowing out of skills and a lack of strategic investment. On another level, these two sections of society are bound together by common values – a longing for stability and recognition, which translates into a concern for more secure, meaningful jobs and an acknowledgement of diverse talents and vocations.

Both groups have overlapping material interests and immaterial values. They vote for a party that offers a sense of common purpose to achieve a transformative agenda, matched by a sense of mutual obligations to deliver it. Both parts of Australian society are attached to their individual rights and freedoms, but they also accept and cherish the fact that they have duties to others – to their families, neighbours, colleagues, and fellow citizens. As part of its struggle for national self-determination, Australia wove a web of personal entitlements and mutual obligations. Binding people together by what Paul Collier calls "the gentle pressure of self-respect and peer esteem".[4] Labor failed to get the balance right and this was an important reason why it did not command majority support in 2019.

The fact that the party did not see the defeat coming is all the more worrying since the signs were abundant. The main problems were known before the election. During the Howard years, Labor lost four federal elections in a row. After one defeat, in 2004, a senior trade union official wrote a hard-hitting assessment of the ALP's predicament that is just as true and relevant now as it was then:

> The principal lesson from four federal election losses is clear: Labor
> has failed to establish its economic management credentials to voters
> in the provincial centres and outer suburbs of metropolitan Australia.
> In an economy driven by record levels of personal, household and
> private sector debt, interest rates and economic management are the
> top vote-changing issues. Economic credibility is a gateway through
> which Labor must pass before it can bring its policy strengths in health
> and education to bear. In 2004, Labor failed to dent the Coalition's

commanding lead as economic managers. Instead, Labor relied on its traditional strengths in healthcare and education, together with a dramatic appeal in environment policy.

In 2019, like in 1998-2004, the party privileged elite progressivist prejudices over secure jobs, which led to the loss of Queensland seats. Labor's messaging resonated in inner-city seats in Sydney and Melbourne. But in Queensland it was a different story. Labor was wedged. The 'progressive dilemma with Queensland characteristics' is arguably the ALP's biggest obstacle to forming government. The ALP was right to focus on low wages but wrong not to put a stronger emphasis on job creation and the aspiration of working Australians in the suburbs.

Connected with an unbalanced policy platform was another fundamental problem – a plethora of policies that superseded and obscured the party's vision of renewal. The same analysis goes on to say this:

> One myth that must be put to rest is that Labor won the last campaign but lost the election. Labor's campaign was both thematically and tactically flawed . . . Labor released a lot of policies with no punch (seventy-six announced during the campaign, and nearly one hundred prior). Most Labor policies received little public attention, while the Coalition relentlessly hammered home a few key messages.

Once again, the parallels with today are striking. The ALP national conference of 2018 approved a platform with an impressive array of policy proposals. In the run-up to the elections the party published detailed costings in relation to some of the key announcements on franking credits and negative gearing. But the myriad of tax increases to fund spending commitments ended up being so complex as to be overwhelming. The new shadow treasurer, Jim

Chalmers, acknowledged this, saying "we couldn't build a big enough constituency for our tax proposals; their complexity left us vulnerable to under-the-radar lies and scares about death duties and pension cuts which couldn't be countered effectively or in time".[5] Indeed, Labor had a lot of explaining to do, which in politics amounts to losing the argument. As Paul Keating remarked about John Hewson's policies in 1993, "If you understood it you wouldn't vote for it, if you don't understand it you shouldn't".

Moreover, the 2004 analysis I have been quoting identifies another fundamental flaw that applied to Labor in 2019:

> There was little political gain in appealing to Green voters when there was no danger of their preferences going to the Coalition. Labor relied too much on preference strategies while its primary vote withered. The big 'L' Left appeals meant that Federal Labor vacated the centre ground for Howard to exploit. In this era of 'conservative populism', the traditional understanding of left-right political discourse is an oversimplification of the Australian electorate. There is also a 'top-down' divide, between highly educated, urban intelligentsia (who, despite Party [*sic*] differences, share similar liberal social values and an economically rationalist acceptance of globalisation) and so-called 'ordinary Australians' in the suburbs and regions (who are risk-averse to economic restructuring and suspicious of liberal social values).

This captures the growing fragmentation of contemporary Australian society and the concomitant political polarisation that takes the 'progressive dilemma' to the next level – the potential collapse of Labor's electoral coalition. In fact, the ALP's traditional electorate is splitting and the party is struggling to hold on to its traditional base without which it cannot a win a popular or parliamentary majority. This point is made powerfully in the following passage from the same document:

Labor's support has been increasingly confined to the Left intelligentsia with its post-Whitlam emphasis on progressive policies on the environment, refugees and multiculturalism. The policy priorities of the Left are not wrong, but they have acquired a prominence that is now a barrier to Labor reconnecting with both its blue-collar base and middle Australia.

So what was – and is – to be done? The document recommends a number of policy areas that should feature prominently in the ALP's offer, notably policy solutions covering affordable housing, vocational training, infrastructure investment, renewable energy, and a "revived national bond market and investment incentives" to unlock new funding streams. All of those policy ideas retain their importance today. But crucially the document insists that Labor needs to hold in balance an attention to economic needs and a concern for questions of meaning and belonging:

> Finally, Labor should reject the theory that people want services rather than tax cuts. Many voters, including members of my union [the Australian Workers' Union], want both. The Hawke and Keating Governments introduced seven different income tax cuts over thirteen years. Labor should support personal income tax cuts and fewer, simpler business taxes. This will send a powerful message of understanding about managing productivity in a competitive economy. The time for short-term fixes is over. Labor's supporters want us to talk dollars as well as sense.[6]

The author of this document is Bill Shorten. The tragedy of his leadership is that he ended up embracing the very progressive politics that alienates sections of the working and middle-class voters who are more socially conservative and want a radically reforming Labor government, which offers working Australians a share of prosperity and the good life. Whereas progressive politics is timid on economic justice but bold on social reform, radical politics is bold on the economy but more moderate about society. Without the support of the working class, the ALP cannot gain and retain power. They are key to the quest for a politics of the common good.

The slide into minority politics: the ALP and the spectre of European social democracy

The crushing defeat in 2019 shows that Australian Labor is not immune from the fate suffered by its social-democratic sister parties. Since the onset of the 2010s, they have all faced a similar situation of losing elections and being out of office. So far the ALP has avoided the demise of many centre-left parties across the West.[7] Over the past ten years or so, social-democratic parties have not just been ejected from power but also fallen to historic lows. The German social democrats won just over 20 percent in the 2017 elections – their lowest vote since 1933 and close to their historic low in 1889. Since renewing the grand coalition with the centre-right Christian Democrats in late 2017, its support collapsed in the polls – overtaken by the Greens. In Italy, the Democratic Party was expelled from office in the March 2018 elections and is currently at about 20 percent in opinion polls. After the elections in September 2018, the Swedish social democrats are the largest party, but their 28 percent is the lowest vote since 1908. Social democracy is rapidly receding in its continental European heartland.

The decline of social-democratic parties is even more dramatic in France, the Czech Republic, Poland, and Ireland where support for the centre-left has fallen to single figures. This mirrors the experience in Greece where the PASOK party tumbled from 44 percent in 2009 to just 5 percent in 2015. Pasokification is now commonly used to describe the collapse of social democracy in the West and the rise of populist parties that are variously more left or right-wing but either way nationalist and protectionist in outlook. The Greek case where the far-left party Syriza governed until July 2019 together with the radical right-wing Independent Greeks-National Patriotic Alliance party demonstrates this realignment. And now the conservatives, New Democracy, rule. Far from being a social-democratic moment, the 2008 financial crash accelerated the decline of the centre left – except in Australia where the ALP under Kevin Rudd and Wayne Swan emerged as responsible stewards of the public finances, while taking bold action to prevent a recession.[8]

Those centre-left parties that are faring somewhat better than continental European social democracy are either out of power or have embraced a form of left populism – or both at once. Hillary Clinton may have beaten Donald Trump in terms of the popular vote in 2016, but her majority of 3 million was concentrated in eight voting districts – four in the state of New York and four in the state of California, both of which are Democrat strongholds. Meanwhile, she lost three 'blue wall' strongholds that had not been won by the Republicans since Reagan: Wisconsin, Michigan, and Pennsylvania. Before and since Trump's victory, the Democratic Party has been deeply divided between the centrist liberalism of Hillary Clinton and the radicalism of Bernie Sanders who nearly beat her to the presidential nomination on a political platform combining a commitment to a more moral (but also much more statist) economy with a defence of progressive patriotism against Clinton's globalist and Trump's nativist identity politics.[9] In the mid-term federal elections in the United States in November 2018, the Democratic Party won a majority in the House of Representatives. But there was no 'blue wave' to put the Democrats on course to defeat Trump in the 2020 presidential contest by building a cross-class and cross-cultural coalition anchored in a story of national renewal. As the American commentator, David Brooks, said:

> After 30 years of multiculturalism, the bonds of racial solidarity trump the bonds of national solidarity. Democrats have a very strong story to tell about what we owe the victims of racism and oppression. They do not have a strong story to tell about what we owe to other Americans, how we define our national borders and what binds us as Americans.[10]

Something similar applies to British Labour which has oscillated between New Labour's free-market capitalism and Jeremy Corbyn's post-Brexit project of 'socialism in one country'. But either way both are committed to forms of open-border cosmopolitanism with little to say about the national bonds binding Britons together.

By contrast, since breaking with the pre-1970s legacy of its support for the White Australia Policy, the ALP has worked hard to avoid racism and promote a form of progressive patriotism.[11] This conception of national identity appeals to both the Indigenous population, including the unique and diverse cultures of Australian Aboriginal and Torres Strait Islander peoples, and immigrants who wish to integrate. In recent years, Labor fought the extremes of globalism and nativism – the latter denotes championing white inhabitants against immigrants. The ALP at its best is in favour of a broad 'radical centre' that is simultaneously left on the economy, work, and welfare, and more moderate on social and cultural issues. (In chapters 2 and 3, I conceptualise this in paradoxical terms as 'radical moderation'.) This is the position of the ALP going back to the governments of Gough Whitlam, Bob Hawke, and Paul Keating.

In 1996, Keating argued that "the market economy's social graft which Labor has put into place" means that "we have the best of all worlds – vitality, diversity, strength, critical mass, and a good economy with the right bases to it, and a cohesive social fabric that makes every Australian feel as though they matter and that they are important".[12] This is the language of a reformer who understood the people. That such an understanding was inconsistently appreciated and, at times, not appreciated enough, is to the tragedy of the modern ALP at the national level.

Since the 1990s and the 2000s, the ALP has become much more socially liberal, which has reduced its capacity to maintain support from more socially conservative working-class voters and thereby secure a majority. This matters particularly at a time when many of those voters have abandoned the centre-left in favour of either the centre-right or even the far-right, as with Front National in France (now National Rally), the United Kingdom Independence Party (UKIP) and now the Brexit Party in Britain, Pauline Hanson's One Nation Party and Clive Palmer's United Australia Party. On the whole, the ALP managed to hold the line on questions of identity without descent to the 'moral panic' that is identity politics.[13] But Labor's lack of appeal among its traditional base remains central to the party's electoral success – as the results in Queensland, in particular, underscore.

Australian Labor resisted left populism in its triple dimensions: first, the economics of statist nationalisation and tech utopia; secondly, the culture of abstract cosmopolitanism; and, thirdly, an anti-Western foreign policy. Arguably, the rise of left populism, such as Greece's Syriza, Spain's Podemos or the British Labour Party under Jeremy Corbyn, seems to have re-energised social democracy.[14] Syriza and Podemos helped the left to retake power amid extreme economic hardship and the neo-liberal straightjacket of the Eurozone. The British Labour Party saw its membership soar to about 500,000; its share of the vote reached over 40 percent in the 2017 election – the highest since Tony Blair's second landslide victory in 2001. But Syriza relied on support from a far-right party in order to govern, while Podemos is not part of the Spanish government led by the socialist party PSOE. Despite Corbyn's constructive ambiguity and his argument in favour of a softer exit from the European Union, Labor's electoral coalition is beginning to split between its more metropolitan middle-class supporters who voted to remain in the EU and the suburban, rural, and coastal communities that voted for Brexit. 'Our friends in the north,' as Londoners refer to the traditional Labour heartland, voted to exit what they saw as a European construct rigged against their interests. Though faced with an unpopular Tory government and ten years of austerity, UK Labour does not look like it can win a parliamentary majority without support from the ultra-progressive Liberal Democrats as well as the nationalists in both Scotland and Wales. So in none of these cases does the insurgent left enjoy majority support in parliament or among the people. The 2019 defeat for the ALP was crushing because of the low primary vote, but the Coalition's primary vote was not outstanding either. That seems to be the message, not that social democracy is on the nose. All major political parties in western democracies are struggling.

In the United States, the Democrats are also out of power, losing elections against candidates with overwhelming weaknesses (Trump) and against centre-right parties split between establishment liberals and libertarian insurgents (the United States' Republicans, which also applies to the British Conservative Party). In an age of anger and upheaval, the mainstream centre-left has failed to mobilise its own electorate. Some of the most disaffected voters – especially the former industrial working-class who once were the backbone of the left – have abandoned social democrats because they know that the left abandoned them. This applies to Donald Trump in key swing-states such as Ohio, Pennsylvania, Michigan or Virginia as much as it does to Theresa May's Tories, who won the Labour 'safe seats' of Walsall North, Stoke-on-Trent South, and Mansfield. Corbyn-led Labour and the Clintonite Democrats lack ideas and 'connection'. They do not know how to regain the trust of their traditional working-class voters who are more socially conservative, while retaining the vote of their middle-class supporters who are more socially liberal. By contrast, the ALP retains the potential to be a social-democratic party that represents a cross-cultural and cross-class coalition anchored in a substantive sense of justice – the 'fair go' that goes beyond economic utility or individual entitlements in the direction of the common good and mutual flourishing.[15] As the next section explains, Labor's ethical purpose distinguishes the party from much of the left across the West.

The ALP's paradoxical politics

There is little doubt that the present predicament of Western social democracy is not simply a periodic crisis but an existential threat. Back in the 1990s and 2000s, a majority of Western governments were centre-left, starting with Bill Clinton and Tony Blair and followed by Lionel Jospin, Romano Prodi, and Gerhard Schröder. Fewer than twenty years later, social democrats are in power in just six Western countries which – except for Spain – are all smaller countries: New Zealand, Portugal, Sweden, Denmark, and Malta. The decline of the centre-left is mirrored in a fundamental shift away from the winning combination that for some time had ensured electoral successes – fusing economic liberalism with social liberalism. For a time in the 1980s and 1990s social democrats tried to mobilise both the working class, who had suffered under the centre-right in the 1980s, and the new affluent middle class, who by the 1990s saw conservative parties as a spent force. The left beat the right at its own game by championing 'global capitalism with a human face'.

Following the demise of Soviet communism, there was a sense that all things were possible. The new-found optimism was captured by the song that accompanied Tony Blair's triumphal march to the door of 10 Downing Street on the morning of his first landslide victory in May 1997: "Things Can Only Get Better". Henceforth, it seemed that globalisation would take precedence over protection, mass immigration over national borders, minority rights over majority norms, supranational integration over the nation-state and a cosmopolitan culture over national identity. But faced with growing levels of economic and cultural insecurity over the past decade, the centre-left's attempt to win by offering yet more modernisation and liberalisation backfired. It turns out that a majority of people do not want more global capitalism and greater cultural change in their everyday existence. Instead, they like to see much greater economic fairness combined with more social stability, which reflects mainstream attitudes that can be described as economically egalitarian and socially small-c conservative.

Another way of conceptualising this is in terms of a paradoxical politics that does not fit the lazy categorization of left and right, that is sceptical of both left liberalism on culture and right liberalism on the economy. What I am arguing for is actually Labor politics at its best. This is to favour a fusion of radical economic justice with a measure of traditional social cohesion. Key to this is "moving beyond statist egalitarianism and small-l liberalism and recognising Labor's rich paradoxical heritage: at once progressive and conservative; radical and traditional; romantic and rational; patriotic and internationalist".[16] By being committed to a form of progressive patriotism and to building an economy that is more ethical and works better for the people, the ALP at its best captures this radical centre in a way that hardly any other social democratic party does at present – with the exception of the Danish Social Democrats who won the elections in June 2019. Its leader Mette Frederiksen appealed to the working class by saying "you didn't leave us; we left you".[17] She won not by ditching core values but by returning to them: radical on the economy by promising higher wages and moderate on social issues by being tougher on economic immigration. Her politics speaks to a yearning for stability and a sense of belonging.

In Australia, as elsewhere, migration, and ethnic and religious diversity provide both dynamism and potential for community conflict. With almost 30 percent of Australians born overseas, popular participation in democratic decision-making is as vital as effective citizenship. Hence the ALP's promotion of a patriotism that balances respect for diversity and difference with integration into a common culture and an appreciation of the 'Australian way of life'. In this manner, Australian Labor still has significant potential to represent majority views.

In a context of increasing ethnic and cultural diversity, the reference to social cohesion and even socially conservative values might surprise.

It is true that a growing number of people in Western countries and elsewhere are socially liberal in many respects. They prefer a fair and open-minded mentality to an insular and bigoted attitude in terms of ethnic diversity, minority rights, and reasonable levels of immigration. A majority also support same-sex marriage and attempts to reduce the inequality gap between men and women. A sizeable majority, however, is also more communitarian and small-c conservative than the mainstream left recognises.[18] This is key to understanding the electorate and, indeed, Labor's traditional support base. Most people, not least many ethnic minorities, choose a fairly traditional family life, want to live in safe, stable places, and are generally sceptical about the pace of change. Even university graduates and professionals who are more liberal and cosmopolitan in their twenties and thirties tend to become culturally more conservative and communitarian as they settle down and get married or are in long-term relationships. They worry far less about high mobility and much more about buying their own house, finding a good school for their children, having access to decent healthcare, and living in relatively stable communities with low levels of crime and a moderate degree of trust and social behaviour.

It is therefore no surprise that when the centre-left's politics is primarily instrumental and economistic, it ends up losing popular trust and power. Social democracy's gamble of relying on global capitalism to share the proceeds of progress has proven more complicated than expected. Economic progress turned out to be far more contingent and reversible – as with declining wages, precarious jobs, and soaring debt levels. The fall in the living standards of Western workers is illustrated by the Elephant Chart, which shows that the world has witnessed a significant rise in income growth for the poorest, the nascent middle classes in emerging markets, and the super-rich, while the West's working and middle classes experienced a squeeze.[19] In March 2017, Paul Keating echoed the ALP's shift away from economic liberalism when he said "since 2008 liberal economics has gone nowhere . . . liberal economics has run into a dead end and has had no answer to the contemporary malaise".[20]

Moreover, the economy and public services, on which social democrats defeated conservatives in the 1990s and 2000s, are not purely material issues but intertwined with questions of belonging, agency, and democracy. People have moved beyond the idea that wealth will trickle down via the free market or that the beneficent big state will help them out. They yearn for a greater degree of autonomy and self-government in their localities and at their workplace. There is a desire for more community, stability, and agency – the power to shape in some meaningful way a person's own everyday life. Far from being 'left behind' or keen to join a new networked global 'multitude', most people also take pride in their family, friends, work, and the places they inhabit.[21] The ALP's commitment to 'mateship' and a 'fair go' for all is a promotion of specifically Australian values that reflect universal principles of work, family, community, country, and a sense of decency. The need to build a cross-class, cross-cultural coalition involves rejecting both liberal centrism and revolutionary utopianism in favour of a paradoxical politics – at once progressive and conservative, rational and romantic, secular and religious, patriotic and internationalist. Whereas Australian Labor tries to hold these values in balance, the centre-left has almost everywhere else come down on one side. This was thought to be on the 'right side of history'. History has now been upended. The model of secular, cosmopolitan, and progressivist politics is in crisis.

If social democracy is failing, then that is in large part because it no longer represents the people it was set up to protect and defend. The centre-left utopia of fusing liberal democracy with open-borders globalisation and welfare states has not survived contact with reality. Already in 2009 one British historian, Tony Judt, who was a passionate social democrat, observed this:

> It is not by chance that social democracy and welfare states have worked best in small, homogeneous countries, where issues of trust and mutual suspicion do not arise so acutely. A willingness to pay for other people's services and benefits rests on the understanding that they in turn will do likewise for you and your children: because they are like you and see the world as you do. Conversely, where immigration and visible minorities have altered the demography of a country, we typically find suspicion of others and a loss of enthusiasm for the institutions of the welfare state.[22]

The Labor-inspired post-war model ushered in by John Curtin and Ben Chifley embodied much of this social-democratic settlement. And for this reason, the bargain by the centre-left since the 1990s of championing global capitalism combined with social justice at home turned out to be a pact with the devil. It not only reinforced the technocratic rationalism that underpins left-wing centralist, statist politics but also created the conditions for the political insurgency, which is fuelled by a sense of both economic dislocation and cultural dispossession. The 'embedded' political economy of social democrats was never compatible with capital and labour mobility that requires the rationalisation of welfare and a downward social mobility based on lower wages for the working class. Over time, insecure employment, wage stagnation and rising costs of living eroded the economic and cultural foundations of the post-war settlement of shared prosperity and social solidarity.

The social contract on which social democracy rests has given way to a fusion of market anarchy with state control that has hollowed out society. This process is compounded by the end of deference, the rise of individualism, the expansion of the consumer society, and now a form of turbo-consumption, coupled with financialisation, globalisation, and the concomitant tensions over nation, identity, and place. Social democracy was grounded in the solidarity and relative stability of the second half of the twentieth century. But now it struggles in the age of upheaval caused by capital flows, mass migration, and digitisation. These developments exacerbate other fundamental shifts, such as an increasing popular distrust of political institutions and the mutation of mass-membership organisations into small elite-dominated cliques. Today's Western societies are characterised by growing interdependence and fragmentation that leaves liberal democracy even more vulnerable to the threat of global terrorism, the assertiveness of authoritarian 'great powers', and the resurgence of fringe extremes.[23]

In short, the centre-left has struggled in a post-1989 world characterised by market fundamentalism, the sharp decline in union density connected with the erosion of working-class identity, mass immigration, and technological change. Most social democrats lack popular trust and struggle to put forward a political and policy platform that balances the interests of workers and business, cities, towns, and rural communities, as well as the indigenous and immigrant populations. Much of the left lacks a clear sense of purpose that can appeal across cultural and class divisions because its language has become predominantly utilitarian and technocratic – a form of liberal abstraction tinged with aggressive secularism. The latter is married to an agenda of promoting rights as individual entitlements that alienates core supporters and some new voters who value sacrifice and contribution. The remainder of the chapter explores how the ALP so far has largely escaped the social-democratic decline and why it nevertheless requires a more radical renewal if it is to live up to its own best tradition of brokering a national politics of the common good.

The ALP's political outlook

Historically, Labor's political positioning is based on an ethical outlook which charts an alternative to the centrist liberalism of mainstream social democrats and to the utopianism of far-left insurgents. To a significant extent, the ALP's emphasis on the 'fair go' frames the party's approach to renewing its philosophical foundations, setting out its policy platform and reforming its own internal party structures. Instead of being a merely rhetorical device, the commitment to protect and promote fairness and the Australian way of life underpins Labor's strategy of broadening its support beyond more liberal-cosmopolitan inner city areas to suburban and rural communities in a way that allows the party to win seats held by the Liberal Party without losing any to the Greens. This historically required less reliance on a single figure – the messianic leader who delivers power – or on the record of past ALP governments – including the Hawke-Keating administration, however important was its legacy in so many respects.

Rather, Labor requires a vibrant contest of ideas within the party and in conversation with the country. Two elements are necessary for such a contest. One is a critical perspective on Labor federal governments in 1983-1996 and 2007-13 and the areas in which they succeeded and failed. The other is to abandon some of the party's worst instincts, including a tendency for technocratic solutions, its default mode of retreating to central bureaucratic rule or mindless modernisation without a sense of ethical purpose. Today this involves above all rejecting liberal market fundamentalism while also resisting the siren calls of far-left economic nationalisation combined with the promise of a tech utopia that will supposedly usher in a post-capitalist economy without work or workers.

Labor's break with the excesses of economic liberalism

In recent decades, Labor is criticised by people at both ends of the political spectrum: by the Marxist and post-Marxist left for supposedly selling out to neo-liberalism and by liberals and libertarians for allegedly being too statist.[24] Both are largely right about each other but wrong about the ALP. Labor tends to have an economic and fiscal policy that is prudent and responsible, avoiding a strategy of high spending based on high debt or high taxes. At the height of the 2008-09 global financial crash, for example, the Rudd government adopted a more clearly Keynesian policy of fiscal expansion to prevent a recession. It also sought – admittedly with less success – to deliver post-crisis fiscal repair while boosting the growth in jobs and GDP.[25] With national debt at less than 10 percent before the global financial crisis, the Labor government decided to borrow $52 billion to keep the financial system going and support Australia's economy. Through a combination of bank guarantees, cash windfalls (e.g. $900 cheques to pensioners) and public works such as building school halls, the ALP averted a slump and, after a short downturn, economic growth picked up again in the second half of 2009.

This strategy marked a certain departure from the economic policy of the Hawke-Keating governments between 1983 and 1996, which championed a new politics of market liberalisation, deregulation, privatisation, free trade, and higher immigration – building on the Whitlam government that had confirmed the party's break with the White Australia Policy. Among the policies that the Hawke-Keating governments enacted were free floating currency exchange rates, selling off state assets, and deregulating a number of sectors.[26] But whereas the Thatcher and Reagan administrations pursued these policies in divisive ways that pitted capital against labour (using state power against the trade unions), the ALP adopted a much more consensual approach: Keating's government stimulated the economy in 1992-96 and it worked with unions via the 'Prices and Incomes Accord' pioneered by the Hawke government. This involved a sustained attempt by the ALP to achieve a better balance of interests between government and the labour movement – reducing inflation and therefore stemming the increase in the costs of living in exchange for wage demand restrictions. Central to the Accord was the idea of a social wage and public commitments to higher expenditure on education and social security.

The Hawke and Keating era was an example of prudent economic management in the spirit of national consensus. But the regressive side of Labor's progressive turn (performed by Whitlam and taken forward by both Hawke and Keating) was its growing reliance on the free market underwritten by the central state. Accordingly, the market would be the main mechanism for free choice and emancipation, with state support for those who cannot help themselves, with state assistance in case of market failure.

After Labor was defeated in 1996, with the Howard government in office, the main problems with the underlying economic and cultural liberalism became clearer. Not just in that it led to higher inequality of income and assets, but also that individual freedom and collective material utility supersede the ALP's commitment to the common good. Nick Dyrenfurth argues that Labor itself was at fault: "Labor embraced a bloodless form of statist liberalism – economic and increasingly social – at odds with its original purpose and orientation towards national tradition and a language fashioned towards the basic aspiration of leading a good, secure and meaningful life: the very reason Labor was put on this earth".[27] There are good arguments, however, for saying that Australian Labor's management of change in the 1980s to the mid-1990s was exceptional compared to any other centre-left administration on the world stage. In contrast, the significant destabilisation of the US industrial base after the North America Free Trade Agreement (NAFTA) under President Clinton in 1994 eventually left some regions devastated with no helping hand by the state. This was not Australia's path to economic reform. In Australia there was significant economic change combined with assistance to the displaced, and the suddenly unemployed. In America the seeds of revolt were sowed in communities that felt that the liberal elites cared not two hoots for them.

Under Shorten's leadership, the ALP sought to restate its ethical purpose by breaking with many aspects of an uncritical economic liberalism. While remaining committed to the Hawke-Keating-era market economy, Labor recognised the excesses of liberalisation in relation to banking, finance, and other sectors where rampant greed and corruption benefitted a certain 'new class' of executive at the expense of workers and the wider society. That is why since August 2016 Shorten pushed for a royal commission into the banking sector, saying that "excessive market power breeds arrogance" and bemoaning "fees, charges, credit card rip-offs, ATM fees and a payment for paper statements".[28] Under public pressure the Liberals, who voted 26 times against a royal commission, relented and the Royal Commission into Misconduct in the Banking, Superannuation and Financial Services Industry was finally established in December 2017. It since discovered corporate corruption linked to the cartel capitalism of the big four banks – Commonwealth, Westpac, NAB, and ANZ – thereby vindicating Labor's stance.

Presented to the Royal Commission was evidence of criminal fraud, forged documents, and asset-stripping that resulted in losses of hundreds of millions of dollars for ordinary people. For example, the financial services company AMP admitted that it charged millions in premiums for life insurance to over 4,500 superannuation customers it knew had died. The big four banks tried to spin the various scandals into stories about a series of unfortunate accidents, including mis-selling products and charging clients fees for no service. When the final report was submitted on 1 February 2019, the Coalition hoped it would bring closure. But there are calls underway for a second commission to more exhaustively uncover the facts, crimes, and misdemeanours. The regulatory authorities were moved to take some action to ban from corporate activity particular directors. Yet despite evidence of fraud and illegal behaviour, the guilty look like escaping criminal prosecution. As occurred with the global financial crisis, 'respectable white collar criminals' escape the full sanction of the law. In spite of more than 10,000 submissions, only 27 customers were given the chance to tell their stories to the commissioner, the Hon. Kenneth Hayne QC. From the outset, the banking commission was hamstrung by its brevity, narrow terms of reference, lack of witnesses, and paucity of resources – a single commissioner assisted by legal counsel. By contrast, the Royal Commission into Institutional Responses to Child Sexual Abuse heard evidence in more than 8,000 private sessions over five years and had seven commissioners on the case, not just one. Under Albanese, the ALP is likely to renew its calls for a second banking commission that focuses on the complaints from customers. And there is a precedent for two royal commissions conducted into the same issue, as was the case with the collision of the HMAS Melbourne with the HMAS Voyager in 1964.

The other element of Shorten's economic proposals that will survive is the focus on slow wage growth and low household consumption. As the new shadow treasurer, Jim Chalmers, argues, many working Australians face not only wage stagnation but also cuts to penalty rates and rising costs of living in relation to childcare and electricity. Labor now focuses on how more money can once again be put in people's pockets, starting with support for the government's first tranche of proposed income tax cuts for low and middle-income earners from 1 July 2019 onwards.[29] Labor's new team is also considering tax cuts for other groups, as part of a larger revamp of economic policy. In a departure from Shorten's rhetoric about the 'top end of town', Albanese already has shifted the emphasis away from a perceived anti-business bias toward ideas that are at once pro-worker *and* pro-business, for example combining higher wages with sensible tax decisions, which means formally opposing the Coalition's proposed tax cuts on higher incomes but not winding back dividend imputation (as the ALP had promised in the 2019 election). According to Albanese, on the latter the party's proposals alienated voters who were just about managing, including retirees who earned a little extra from franking credits – first introduced by the Hawke government when Keating was Treasurer. Albanese said that those voters "felt as though we weren't giving them respect and that we were classifying them as wealthy, but they weren't wealthy. We need to learn the mistakes and listen to what they're saying".[30]

Speaking to the Labor caucus in the first days of his leadership, Albanese insisted on the importance of linking individual aspiration to shared interests that are anchored in a common purpose. For him, the promise of both the party and the country is the

> opportunity to aspire to a better life. But it's not just about individualism, because I believe Australians firmly want not just a better life for themselves, they want a better life for their family, they want a better life for their neighbours, they want a better life for their community and for their nation. And that's what Labor offers. That's what we need to clearly articulate.[31]

In economic terms, this means championing growth and secure and meaningful jobs, as well as support for small and medium-sized enterprise. In Albanese's words, "Labor supports economic growth as the core part of our agenda, because jobs are always first, second, and third priority of this great party".[32] Key to fulfilling the promise of a common purpose is a proper balance between market fundamentalism and statist control. Chapter 4 outlines a series of policy ideas in this direction.

Labor's patriotism and distancing from identity politics

Besides breaking with many aspects of crude economic liberalism, the other way in which the ALP can be true to Labor's original ethical outlook is in relation to national identity and the country's role in the world. One of the fundamental threats to an ALP majority position is the temptation of left-progressivist identity politics in opposition to a right-wing politics of fear pedalled by One Nation and elements in the Coalition who have promoted division over issues of immigration and asylum. The ALP's history on these questions has many dark stains – from the White Australia Policy to the most controversial aspects of the mandatory detention policy introduced by the Keating government. However, there is little doubt that Labor has moved in a much more moderate direction on most matters. For many decades it has championed multiculturalism, an individual rights agenda, and a whole host of policies of non-discrimination on grounds of race, gender, religion, sexuality, disability, or age. On most issues, the ALP, broadly speaking, is a socially liberal party.

At the same time, Labor is also a party that defends patriotism, seeks to balance individual rights with mutual obligations, and combines a commitment to diversity and inclusion with an emphasis on solidarity and community. Social liberalism and cultural patriotism are in tension with each other and they require some trade-offs and difficult compromises. This is because the liberal emphasis on individual rights and freedoms clashes with a patriotic accentuation of obligations to others and love for the country – in short, the primacy of 'me' over 'we'. The ALP attempts to hold in balance individual identity and the national community by suggesting that the foundational principles of freedom, equality, and democracy involve a degree of loyalty, duty, and sacrifice for the building of a common life. Shorten called it "that covenant of trust that each successive generation will have regard for the next",[33] and Albanese speaks of "common interests and common purpose":

> Bob Hawke showed us, I believe, that we're at our best when we bring the nation together. And that needs to be a guiding light for us. Bringing people together. Trying to do what we can, even from opposition, but then in government, to narrow the gap, to say to

Australians, that what divides us is much less than what unites us. That we do have common interests and we do have common purpose.[34]

To build a freer, more equal, and more democratic country requires both leadership and popular participation in power. Leadership is about binding up the wounds of past divisions, over conscription for example, and building a new settlement, as Labor did in the 1940s, and again in the 1980s and early 1990s. Greater popular participation in decision-making will require a wide range of reforms – from more workplace power via community and neighbourhood-based institutions to the functioning of federal and state governments. These are outlined in more detail in chapter 4.

For the ALP, regaining people's trust involves a broad alliance of class, culture, and creed anchored in a shared national story. As the work of Tim Soutphommasane suggests, Labor's patriotism should not primarily be legal because that would mean restricting it to a transactional exchange of rights and responsibilities.[35] Nor does a form of revolutionary republican patriotism have much appeal; this can slide into blood and soil atavism that would continue to exclude Aboriginal and Torres Strait Islander people – and Labor has a deeply problematic history of promoting the White Australia Policy. Rather, the ALP – at its best – promotes progressive patriotism, which is cultural in nature and seeks to celebrate a more cohesive narrative of national identity through the country's key institutions – federal and state parliaments, schools, civic associations, and the media. This involves shifting the emphasis from a discourse of individual opportunities to common learning based on education and the teaching of national history and from assimilation to acculturation to national culture along with the integration of minority migrant perspectives in public institutions and practices. As the ALP's national platform puts it:

> Our national unity is based on mutual respect, shared values and a
> commitment to work together to build a stronger Australia. . . .
> Australia's diversity is a source of national strength and a critical factor
> in nation building. Labor supports a multicultural society underpinned
> by Australian citizenship and respect of Australian values and will
> maintain non-discriminatory migration policies and respect the
> heritage and customs of migrants.[36]

This means a difficult balancing between a proper safeguarding of national borders and national interests, on the one hand, and treating "people seeking our protection with dignity and compassion and in accordance with our international obligations, the rule of law and core Australian principles of fairness and humanity".[37] To achieve such a balance, the ALP promises to limit mandatory detention to 90 days and to make conditions in the detention centres more humane. The other aspect of this balance is improving access to citizenship:

> Australia should encourage all permanent residents to become citizens.
> Labor's citizenship process will focus on the principles underlying
> Australia's citizenship pledge: Australia's democratic beliefs and laws,
> and the rights, responsibilities and privileges of Australian citizenship.
> Australian citizenship is a critical part of encouraging participation
> in the Australian community. Labor will remove unnecessary and
> unintended barriers to citizenship, particularly for vulnerable groups
> of migrants.[38]

Greater economic justice and more social cohesion are part of the same struggle for a more economically and culturally secure country. Kim Beazley embodied this position. In 2001, he said this:

> We've looked down through the fog of war to the kitchen table
> of the average Australian family. To those who sit around it, we've

listened to their hopes and their dreams, the aspirations that they
have for their young folk that they get a decent education, the
aspirations and concerns that they have to ensure that they have
access to affordable health care. Their love of the future of this
nation, a nation where people don't leave when they have bright
ideas, but come here when they have bright ideas.[39]

The fight for a progressive patriotism – coupled with a defence,
security, and foreign policy that emphasises both internationalism and
the patriotic defence of national interest through cooperation, as set
out by Beazley – indicates that compared with the centre-left across
the West, Australian Labor is less liberal-cosmopolitan and more
small-c conservative and communitarian: concerned with obligations
to community and country rather than simply being interested in
individual rights. This is underpinned by a conception of justice
anchored in a working philosophy of the common good, as I argued
in the introduction, which reflects the influence of the social justice
tradition of the churches and is at the heart of Labor's understanding
of its ethical purpose.

Lessons from defeat

The ALP has to learn hard lessons from the loss in 2019. The first and
most important is that Labor cannot win without cultivating working
class support. Rather than staking its platform on workers and their
jobs, Labor instead defended a narrow position on climate change
that appealed largely to middle-class voters. In Queensland, the
party's ambiguity over the controversial Adani coalmine backfired. By
attempting to be all things to all people, the party lost core working-
class voters who care primarily about safe and meaningful jobs, so that
they can feed themselves and their families and get social recognition

for their contribution. And what goes for regional seats in Queensland also applies to a host of suburban seats across the country.

Secondly, the centre-left needs a strong narrative that binds together economic and cultural concerns. Progressive themes such as climate change, equality, and the inclusion of minorities are key in the battle against the Greens and some independent candidates, but alone they do not deliver a popular or parliamentary majority. If it is to prevail against the Coalition, Labor needs to speak to small-c conservative values of belonging to community and country. In an age of insecurity, people desire a measure of stability and cohesion. They do not want their lives or the places they inhabit to change radically unless it serves their wellbeing in tangible ways.

Thirdly, the ALP needs to listen to, and understand, the people who did not vote for Labor, rather than blaming their leader, their election programme, campaign headquarters, or their opponents in politics and the media. This is particular true in the contest against the far-right populism of One Nation and the new United Australia Party led by Clive Palmer. Immediately after the results, Labor MPs and Senators rushed to blame Palmer and his multi-million-dollar advertising campaign for the party's defeat. Or else they accused the Murdoch press and Coalition 'scare campaign' slogans for destroying Shorten. Blaming others is part of the denial involved in dealing with loss. But it obscures the fundamental task required of the party if it wants to win in 2022.

The ALP lacks a strong story that connects with people's values – economic justice but also social cohesion at a time of unprecedented upheaval.

Fourthly, Labor requires leadership that embodies the party's purpose of defending both the labour interest and the national interest.

Shorten was ultimately more of a party figure than a popular leader, but his great merit was uniting Labor after internal coup and counter-coup during the years of the former Labor prime ministers Kevin Rudd and Julia Gillard, which ended with the party's ejection from power in 2013. Under Shorten, the ALP developed a robust policy platform, but it failed to win back working-class support and broaden its appeal to some of its other former core voters, such as people of faith, including large numbers of Catholics who have migrated to the Liberals. By contrast, Scott Morrison not only held a divided Liberal and National Coalition together, he also successfully projected the image of a strong national leader. Morrison dedicated his election victory to the 'quiet Australians' who work hard and care for their families. While the message was populist in tone, it cut through the white noise of technocracy and social media. After a muddled ALP campaign that failed to focus much, still less on restoring the promise of a 'fair go', Morrison parked the Liberals' tanks firmly on Labor territory. In his victory speech, the prime minister declared, "We're going to get back to work for the Australians that we know go to work every day, who face those struggles and trials every day. They're looking for a fair go and they're having a go and they're going to get a go from our Government". To lose is one thing. For Labor to see its rhetoric appropriated by the Liberals is an added humiliation.

To reclaim the fair go, Labor needs to renew its public philosophy of the common good – providing everyone a share in those things that make life worth living. A commitment to the common good is about pursuing personal fulfilment while meeting our obligations to one another and the wider society. This provides a richer conception of justice than the Coalition's policy of maximising utility and promoting individual freedom. Labor's ethical purpose helps the party to address not just economic injustice but also social fragmentation and cultural instability. Migration, together with ethnic and religious diversity, provide both dynamism and potential for community conflict. With almost 30 percent of Australians born overseas, popular participation in democratic decision-making is as vital as effective citizenship education and the instilling of a sense of civic duty.

Hence the ALP's promotion of patriotism that balances respect for diversity and difference with integration into a common culture and an appreciation of the Australian way of life – mateship and a fair go for all. These specifically Australian values reflect universal principles of work, family, community, country, and a sense of decency. To broker a national politics of the common good, Labor needs to resolve the tension between its centralised structure and a more diverse country. The electorate is split into more socially progressive, urban, and university-educated middle-class voters and a more socially conservative, often regional working class, whose support the ALP needs in order to win. The need to build a cross-class, cross-cultural coalition involves rejecting both liberal centrism and revolutionary utopia in favour of a paradoxical politics – at once progressive and conservative, romantic and rational, secular and religious, patriotic and internationalist. If Labor wants to gain and retain office to govern in the national interest, it needs to be intellectually prepared for government after the next election. This requires a critical sense of where it has come from and where it is going. The following chapter charts the history of how the ALP has understood its ethical purpose, which traditions have influenced it, and how the party lost its moral compass.

2

Past
A short history of
Labor's ethical purpose

Paradox and myth

The ALP's paradoxical disposition of being both a radical and a small-c conservative party reflects to a significant degree Australia's history and the distinctive character of the Australian people. Binary distinctions such as bushmen versus city-dwellers, ex-convicts versus free persons, pious versus irreverent, can be misleading. They fail to capture the people's past experiences and their sense of shared identity, including a love of the land, an attachment to work and to the family, affection for mates, scepticism about authority, and opposition to privilege.[1] Such and similar sentiments are as progressive and egalitarian as they are traditional and communitarian, and they shaped the early labour movement from which the ALP gradually emerged.

In turn, the birth and evolution of the Labor Party contributed to, and continues to mirror, Australia's national story – a story of nation-building anchored in the lives of ordinary people rather than the privileged elites represented by other parties. Graham Freudenberg, a speechwriter for ALP leaders Arthur Calwell, Gough Whitlam, and Bob Hawke, said that "more than any other political party in the world, the Australian Labor Party reflects and represents the character of the nation which produced it".[2] This is echoed by Paul Keating (whose speeches were not written by Freudenberg), who once declared about the ALP: "We are the people who make Australian history . . . our party sets the ethos of Australia".[3]

This chapter explores how the ALP has historically understood the Australian ethos and the party's own ethical outlook, first in the period from its inception to John Curtin and from Ben Chifley, then under Gough Whitlam, and finally during the premierships of Bob Hawke and Paul Keating. The reason for focusing on the ALP's prime ministers is because their leadership commanded both party and popular support in ways that often transcend the binary opposites of Labor's left and right factions. Curtin, for example, embodied in several ways Labor's paradoxical disposition, evolving as he did from being a fervent champion of anti-militarist socialism to being a patriotic wartime leader. Even though he died too early to build a post-war national settlement, his leadership set Australia on its course to becoming a key pillar of the Western alliance. He also bequeathed a Labor Party that overcame two major splits – over conscription during World War I and over Jack Lang's economic plan during the Great Depression. Curtin's politics combined patriotism with internationalism and economic radicalism with fiscal rectitude.

More generally, as Nick Dyrenfurth writes, the ALP's disposition "was always informed by small 'c' conservatism and other traditions such as Catholic social teaching, non-conformist religions and localised institutions of working-class self-help. Appealing to such a disposition remains relevant to Labor's approach to many issues from job security, workplace power, automation as well as climate change and universal healthcare".[4] The chapter shows that when the ALP abandons its paradoxical disposition in favour of a single identity – such as liberal or progressive – it tends to lose its distinct ethical purpose and with it the wider national ethos.

To make this argument, the chapter discusses a number of myths about the ALP that continue to dominate both academic research and public debate about the party's soul. First of all, that Labor was strongly Catholic until about the 1960s and that therefore it was an integral part of the sectarianism in Australian politics.[5] This forgets that the ALP only became more strongly Catholic in the mid-1910s over the question of conscription, and that from the outset Labor was a party of reconciling estranged interests – between Protestants and Catholics, between rural and urban workers as well as between the labour interest and the interest of capital owners.[6] While sectarian divisions beset both Australia and the Labor Party for many decades, it is equally true that the social justice tradition of the churches was instrumental in helping the ALP and the wider labour movement to build bridges between different communities and groups. In other words, Catholic social teaching and comparable traditions in Anglicanism and the Nonconformist churches tempered the sectarian divisions, as well as the ideological clash or power battle between the party's left and right factions.

Connected with this point is a second myth – that Labor was supposedly a bourgeois capitalist workers party, not a popular socialist workers party, and that this requires a break with all the forces preventing a far-left revolutionary politics.[7] Tellingly, this claim neglects the crucial role of pastoral workers and miners in regional communities in creating and developing the Labor Party. Any narrative on Australian Labor needs to appreciate a salient insight: for Labor to be successful, there is the need to command support from more socially conservative blue-collar workers and regional communities, who are always important to the ALP winning a majority. For example, Andrew Fisher, the first Labor prime minister to gain a popular majority in 1910, offered a certain brand of democratic socialism that was as economically egalitarian and internationalist as it was socially traditional and patriotic.

To assert that Labor was bourgeois rather than popular also fails to recognise the party's historic transformative project of "civilising capitalism" and turning the capitalist system into a more moral market economy.[8] This was a key characteristic of the ALP's ethical orientation in the post-1945 era, including the Chifley and Whitlam governments, as well as the commitment to the Accord and the implementation of a social wage during the Hawke-Keating years. As the 1907 *Harvester Case* illustrates, the entire edifice of industrial relations draws on the social teaching of the Catholic Church, such as embedded cooperation between workers and employers, and the distributist tradition of giving more land or private property to workers.

Building on this, the third myth concerns the party's apparent evolution towards an ever-greater progressive left-wing outlook by jettisoning its more conservative inclinations. But this does not understand the need for balancing rival values and interests, or Labor's commitment to a path of 'radical moderation', which fuses economic egalitarianism with social stability in order to command majority support. Gough Whitlam's leadership is a good example of how Labor combined a radical reforming strategy in terms of policy and party change (including a greater appeal to new voters) with more traditional causes, such as strengthening the power of ALP parliamentarians and advocating a 'needs basis' for state aid for Catholic and other faith-based schools. One potentially interesting candidate 'who got away' was The Rev. Alan Walker, one of the greatest of Australian Christian leaders. Prior to the 1969 federal election, Whitlam approached Walker to consider running for Labor. Walker was then a Methodist Minister and instigator-founder in 1963 of Lifeline, the non-denominational volunteer crisis centre which, provides suicide prevention services, mental health support, and emotional assistance, via telephone, face-to-face, and online assistance – saving the lives of many thousands. But Walker felt more comfortable in Christian ministry than serving in the political arena for the party he had always voted for.[9] The approach by Whitlam showed he was attuned to reach out and form the broadest possible winning coalition – including with religious folk who were naturally aligned with Labor.

Far from simply taking a secular progressivist turn, Labor under Whitlam managed to heal some of the wounds opened by the split with the DLP through regaining the support of some sections of the Catholic community that, like Whitlam himself, were more middle-class and small-l liberal. Crucially, he was able to win a majority without relying on support from the right-wing Catholics associated with B. A. Santamaria and the Movement he headed. At the same time, it is true that both main political parties – and even the churches in Australia – came to be dominated by the tensions between a more liberal and a more conservative outlook. The old religious sectarianism mutated into the left-liberal progressive versus right-conservative opposition which is still influential to this day. One example is the divergence between the conservatism of a large part of the Catholic hierarchy and the progressivism of parish priests such as Father Ted Kennedy.[10]

Which Labor? Whose ethos? The ALP's formative years

Australian Labor is one of the oldest and most distinctive social democratic parties in the world. While the German SPD and the Spanish socialist party were founded a few years earlier, the ALP can claim a longer history of continuous political activity anchored in the labour movement with its roots in the 1850s. The Labor Party's history is equally characterised by long continuities and profound ruptures. The tension between industrial and political labour accounts for the unique character of the party: in the early formative years and again in recent decades, the party's main struggle has been to combine the labour interest with the national interest. Between 1891 and 1905, for example, a battle for Labor's soul raged among different groups, including various trade unions, socialist leagues, and public figures, over the party's alternative to the individualism of the capitalist system and the collectivism of communist rivals. The influence of the social justice tradition of the Catholic Church was key in setting the ALP on a path of 'radical moderation' – a commitment to radical reform in the economy combined with building broad popular support based on social stability.[11]

Central to this paradoxical combination was the blending of material with spiritual values as promoted by Catholic social teaching, distributism as well as cognate traditions in Anglicanism and the Nonconformist churches.[12] Binding them together is a commitment to a just social order and greater economic democracy based on a more widespread distribution of property, the living wage, just prices, and worker participation in both enterprise management and the wider economy through cooperative and mutualist arrangements. James Murtagh, in his study on Catholicism in Australia, summarises the mission of Catholic social teaching as "Property for the People" and "the reorganisation of society in vocational groups or guilds representing all interests concerned with the industry [which] would enable worker-owners to plan economic activity, ensure and promote widespread ownership and build an economic democracy within the framework of the existing political democracy".[13] The twin ends of civilising capitalism and democratising politics is what the social justice tradition of the churches and the labour movement have in common, and together they are the roots of the ALP.

What emerged over time from the long-standing relationship between the Christian churches and the labour movement was a specific notion of justice that shifts the emphasis from individual rights and collective utility to the common good. The common good can be defined as an ordering of relationships in a way that holds in balance individual fulfilment with mutual flourishing based on the dignity and equality of all people, which involves both a materially secured and meaningful life. This is historically what Labor promised to provide. Going back to the eight-hour day movement in the 1850s and the Great Strikes in 1890-91, the struggle of organised labour was not confined to economic progress and social advancement but extended to deeper questions about the distribution of power and how to ensure that all citizens can have a "share in those things that make life worth living".[14] Ever since then, the Labor Party's ethical purpose was underpinned by a distinct conception of the good life, anchored in the everyday experience of working people. Work is at the heart of the good life because it is at once a source of income and meaning. In his book on Australian religious thought, Wayne Hudson notes that "Australia's first cardinal, Cardinal Moran (1830-1911) from Sydney, took up Leo XIII's encyclical *Rerum Novarum* of 1891, recognising the dignity and rights of workers and the socialism of the Labor Party when this was almost unprecedented in the Catholic world".[15] The Cardinal knew his Pope well, as the latter in 1852 as Archbishop Pecci was one of Moran's doctoral examiners at the Urban College of Propaganda Fide.

The importance of the ALP's roots in the labour movement *and* in the social justice tradition of the churches is hard to overstate. From the outset, Australia's trade unions brought together urban and rural workers in a common struggle for economic justice and political representation led by the Australian Labor Federation. William Guthrie Spence, leader of the Shearers' Union – then the largest union associated with the Australian Labor Federation – who had united the scattered pastoral unions, famously said that "Unionism came to the Australian Bushman as a religion. It came bringing salvation from years of tyranny".[16] This reflected his religious conviction, including involvement in the temperance movement and his activities as an active Presbyterian. Spence sometimes also preached with the Primitive Methodists and Bible Christians.[17]

The unions, however, were divided between more militant and more moderate members, and the Great Strikes of 1890-91 marked a bitter defeat. Union leaders and workers were jailed, and unions were bankrupted and some outlawed altogether, while non-union labour was used to break industrial action wherever possible. In the subsequent period of economic depression, soaring unemployment meant that competition for jobs was so intense as to strip trade unions of their ability markedly to influence wages or working conditions. This was a colossal rout, which undid much of the progress since the birth of the labour movement in the 1850s. But out of this defeat was born the ALP. The repressive legislation and political hostility towards trade unions prompted organised labour to enter the political fray, fight elections, and gain parliamentary representation in order to shape both law-making and the wider political process.

From the ashes of defeat emerged a political party that transformed the labour movement from spectator to major participant in politics by taking on the two-party system dominated by the Free Trade Party and the Protectionist Party, which gradually merged to form what much later became the Liberal Party.* In this process, the start-up Labor Party assumed not only the mantle of radicalism previously worn by many Free Traders but also the small-c conservatism of regional workers, small farmers, rural hands, and the industrial working class once represented by the Protectionists. As Spence said, "Every tradesman in the colony had an interest in his fellow-tradesmen, however dissimilar their respective callings might be".[18]

---

* Interestingly, the radical new Liberals led by Deakin, from Victoria, were protectionists, whereas the NSW free traders were also liberals who saw protection as ultimately favouring inefficient industries. The division on such questions in non-Labor ranks was intense. With Labor splitting over conscription, the Commonwealth Liberal Party incorporated a number of Labor Party dissidents to form the Nationalist Party of Australia in 1917, which in turn merged with more breakaway Labor politicians to create the United Australia Party in 1931. Under the leadership of Robert Menzies, the UAP became the Liberal Party, whose origins are very different from those of the contemporary United Australia Party led by Clive Palmer. Indeed, when the Liberal Party was founded in 1944, Menzies declared: "We took the name 'Liberal' because we were determined to be a progressive party, willing to make experiments, in no sense reactionary".

The astonishing success of labor candidates with union support in the 1891 elections in New South Wales changed Australian politics profoundly, propelling a new party to a position where it held the balance of power precisely because it occupied a radical centre beyond the hitherto dominant dividing lines of free trade versus protection of the domestic economy in a country riven by religious and social divisions. As the historian Frank Bongiorno explains: "In the culture of colonial unionism, [often] the ideal man was not the nomadic bushman of the Australian Legend, but the respectable breadwinner who showed self-restraint in the interests of his family and his own future prospects".[19] Connected with this was a predominant Protestant Ascendancy and a tribalised Catholic working class primarily of Irish descent but also some Italians and other groups.[20] In response, Labor tried to offer a paradoxical politics of fusing economic redistribution with social cohesion and more political pluralism with greater national unity.

Much of the party's history is an unstable balance between these partly overlapping and partly divergent goals. And like most history, this was by no means a linear evolution. On the contrary, between the foundation of the ALP in 1891 and the federal government led by the first Labor prime minister, John Christian Watson, in 1904, there was an intense battle over the party's soul pitting moderate members against extremist intellectuals, including Christians of different denominations against people of no particular faith and militant atheists. The political contest involved a number of political platforms oscillating between statist socialism and more mutualist solutions, which grew out of the tensions between Labor and various socialist movements. Among the first such movements was the Australian Socialist League, a direct descendant of the First

International, which sought to ally itself with the young ALP and impose a secular philosophy on Labor's first platform of 1891. Even when this development was averted, the years 1893-97 saw the rise of young socialists under the influence of the Second International who attempted to redirect the party away from radical moderation towards extreme ideology and the promise of an explicitly socialist objective.

Between 1898 and 1901, however, the ALP reverted to a more moderate path. Moderates endeavoured to control the Left of the party while, at the same time, they established a Right wing. For example, the platform in the 1901 federal elections included more left-wing calls to introduce compulsory arbitration of industrial disputes and a citizen army (instead of conscription), but also a strident commitment to the White Australia Policy, which was a terrible stain on the party's history until Whitlam's leadership changed it in the late 1960s and his government finally abolished the policy for the whole country on election in December 1972 (building on prime ministers Menzies' and Holt's more progressive conservatism). In the years from 1891 until 1901, there were arguably three Labor parties: the first that resisted any alliance with the Australian Socialist League, the second that worked with the socialists of the Second International in a temporary alliance in 1893-97, and the third that broke links with state socialism and embraced the earlier radical moderation which it developed in the direction of a party that sought to represent both the labour interest and the national interest.

Perhaps the best illustration of Labor's radical moderation was the so-called First Objective agreed at the 1905 Federal Labor Conference. The party committed itself to securing "the full results of their industry to all producers by the collective ownership of monopolies, and the extension of the industrial and economic functions of the

State and Municipality"[21] without pledging, however, to replace free-market capitalism with centralised state socialism. Labor's more mutualist ethical socialism eschewed both incremental change and wholesale revolution in favour of systemic transformation in line with the foundational institutions of family, community, country, and faith. Patrick Ford wrote in his study of the relationship between the ALP and Cardinal Moran that "During this period [1889 and 1907], moderation was given pertinent expression in 1905 with the incorporation into Labor's first objective of the cultivation of an Australian sentiment (something which reflected Moran's persistent advocacy of patriotism)".[22] The formulation encapsulated the tension between the more mutualist and the more monist dimension of Labour's nation-building ethos: "the cultivation of an Australian sentiment based upon the maintenance of racial purity and the development . . . of an enlightened and self-reliant community".[23] The monism of racial purity was a constituent element of the ALP, but so too was its commitment to building a new national community that gave the hitherto disenfranchised people liberty and equality based on worker solidarity.

Nor was Labor's radical moderation a veneer to gloss over irreconcilable contradictions. Rather, as the historian Manning Clark has written, "Labor wore many coats. It was the party of evolution rather than revolution. It was also the party of paradoxes . . . Labor had decided that to obtain political power in a capitalist society, it must make a broad appeal".[24] Indeed, the paradoxical blending of radical and small-c conservative ideas that shaped the ALP in its formative years did translate into radical reforms embodied by the Fisher government, especially after winning a majority in both houses of parliament in the 1910 elections. Among the main measures was, first of all, the creation of a people's bank (the Commonwealth Bank of Australia) as well as actions to dismantle land monopolies and help small-scale farmers by legislating for a land tax. The Fisher government also regulated working hours, wages, and employment conditions, and it improved workers' access to the arbitration system, including Commonwealth industrial and agricultural workers. As Prime Minister in 1910 Fisher lowered the pension age for women from 65 to 60, while also putting in place a maternity allowance that enabled doctors to attend more births and thereby reduced the rate of infant mortality. Confronted with the threat of growing Japanese militarism, the Fisher government implemented a programme for compulsory military training (though not conscription for overseas service) and established the Royal Australian Navy. Fisher's brand of democratic socialism was as economically egalitarian and internationalist as it was socially traditional and patriotic.

At the heart of the struggle over the party's soul in the early years was the influence of the social justice tradition of the churches, which turned out to be instrumental in keeping the ALP on a path of radical moderation. This was vital with Labor's fight against radical groups that believed direct action rather than political reforms would improve the lot of workers. One such group was the Industrial Workers of the World who had grown out of anarcho-syndicalism in the United States and the belief that only a general strike could overthrow the capitalist order. Against revolutionary zeal and ideological puritanism, Catholic social teaching helped to provide the Labor Party with an ethical purpose of radical reform that aimed at reconciling estranged interests, above all capital and labour – with an emphasis of balancing rights with obligations, the dignity of workers with free enterprise, and the fraternity of intermediary institutions with the freedom of democracy and the equality of citizenship. The principles and practices of Catholic social teaching were promoted by the Church hierarchy, in particular Cardinal Moran, Archbishop of Sydney from 1894 to 1911, and Dr Daniel Mannix, Archbishop of Melbourne from 1917 to 1963.

Lay leadership was no less important, based on a variety of intermediary institutions close to the labour movement. In the 1930s onwards those included organisations such as the Campion Society (1929-39), the National Catholic Rural Movement, the Australian National Secretariat of Catholic Action and the Young Christian Workers.[25] Catholic laymen such as the influential Melbourne Campion Society members Frank Maher, Kevin Kelly, Gerard Heffey, Denys Jackson, Murray McInerny, and B. A. Santamaria, as well as the Young Christian Workers activists Ted Long, Bob Maybury, Frank McCann, and Leon Magree identified Catholic and Labor principles as complementary and aligned.[26] For example, through its influence on Santamaria and other opinion formers, the Campion Society was able to disseminate some of the tenets of Catholic social teaching and distributism. As Robert Murray writes, "the Campions looked for distinctly Catholic solutions to the distress of the 1930s in Papal Social Encyclicals and other Catholic social teaching, such as institutionalised cooperation between workers and employers and more land or private property for the workers. The young Campions saw such policies as the practical alternative to communism".[27] And there was a natural home to pursue their thinking – the Australian Labor Party.

The spectre of communism also animated the Catholic hierarchy, notably Moran and Mannix, to ensure that the ALP's more moderate outlook would prevail. The contest for support between extremists and Labor moderates emerged well before the more debilitating threat of communism insinuated from the 1920s onwards. On the Catholic church's role generally in Cardinal Moran's time, it is instructive to quote Patrick Ford at some length:

> The importance of the role of the Catholic element in Labor . . . is clear. It insured support for the moderate tradition in the party, and, as previously, the Catholic element would sustain the endeavour to give a moderate orientation to a Socialist-tinged Platform . . . while Liberals argued for a freedom which took the form of free economic activity and 'freedom of contract', Moran sought a freedom for the worker which was based on property ownership by the workers, and on trade unions whose worker members were free from unfair pressure by unions, employer or State. And while the trade unions were primarily concerned with asserting the rights of the unions rather than their members and proclaiming the duties of employers and the State, Moran insisted on the duty of trade unions to respect the consciences of their members, and on the duty of the State to respect the autonomy of its component societies, including the trade unions. In short, Moran sought to call into being a pluralistic social and political democracy. On the one hand, he advocated just wages, social services and a wide distribution of the ownership of property; on the other, autonomous benefit societies, free and responsible trade unions and the federation of the States with due respect for their essential rights.[28]

The temporising, moderate, yet non-quietist approach of the Church in Australia was distinctive. Church and Labor influenced each other on the issues of the day – without either losing their independence.

In relation to Mannix, it is crucial to remember that his commitment to Catholic social teaching led him to promote positions that were economically egalitarian and socially moderate. Soon after arriving in Melbourne in 1913, he decided to address the long-standing injustice that Catholic schools did not receive state funding, saying that this was "the one great stain upon the statue books of this free and progressive country".[29] At the same time as demanding educational justice, Mannix enjoined his fellow Catholics to "put Australia first and the Empire second", which was partly patriotic and partly aimed at supporting the Irish struggle for Home Rule.

However much this was part of the endemic religious sectarianism in Australia, it is nonetheless the case that social Catholicism was at the heart of the Labor Party and its fight to improve the lot of working people. Not only that: the Christian influence on the ALP extended beyond Catholic social teaching. Anglicans, Evangelicals, Presbyterians, and Methodists were notably active in politics and society, not least women's organisations such as the Women's Suffrage League. They advocated radical social reform in the fields of education, health, land ownership, culture, Aboriginal welfare, cooperative banks, and mutual aid institutions, as well as homes for orphans, the blind, the aged, and the dying. Greater economic justice and more democracy across the country were rallying points between Christian and non-Christian advocates of radical reform.[30]

At the heart of social reform in Australia was Evangelical Christianity, the 'vital religion' driving public policy through William Wilberforce and his fellow believers. To this day, it remains one of the main contributions to the nation's prosperity, as Stuart Piggin and Robert Linder have shown.[31] The Evangelicals not only helped to temper the colonial settlement dominated by convicts, alcohol, and male misogyny by opening up opportunities for women in the economy and society. They also extended care and solidarity to children and youth, and sought to provide protection to the Indigenous population, educating the settlers, and reminding them about the terrible treatment of Aboriginal and Torres Strait Islander people. Then, as now, Evangelical Christians were responsible for much of the welfare for the country's most disadvantaged, and their influence extended beyond the ALP to the more progressive conservatism of the Liberal Party led by Robert Menzies. In the words of Hudson, "evangelical Christians decisively shaped Australia's nation, its values and institutions, although it did so in interaction with other Christian, social utilitarian and secularist tendencies".[32] But while the influence of the Christian social justice traditions was important, it could not prevent internal tensions about how to tackle deep-seated poverty and the imbalance of power, or the growing contradictions between the national interest and the labour interest in the run up to 1914 and the World War One crisis. The next quarter of a century would be marked by two splits, over conscription and over economic policy, which left Labor deeply divided as it struggled to remain faithful to its original purpose of representing both the labour and the national interest.

Two splits and three parties

Andrew Fisher, the radical reforming Labor leader who served as prime minister in the years 1910-13, entered the election campaign in July 1914 with a promise that would be remembered throughout the First World War: "should the worst happen after everything has been done that honour will permit, Australians will stand beside our own to help and defend her [Britain] to our last man and our last shilling".[33] Labor's claim to embody patriotic loyalty rested on the creation of a compulsory military training programme and the Royal Australian Navy. But after victory at the polls and Fisher's return to power, there were groups that were increasingly uneasy about Australia's involvement in what was seen by many as imperial Europe's war. On the left of the party, growing numbers objected that workers had all to lose and nothing to gain from the slaughter between the militaristic and imperialist nations of the northern hemisphere. Eventually, the war effort abroad and economic conditions at home merged into a crisis of political management: the sacrifice on the battlefield and galloping inflation, coupled with a wage freeze imposed by the Labor government, provoked opposition to the leadership of the parliamentary party by both radical groups such as the Industrial Workers of the World (IWW) and trade unions including the Australian Workers' Union (AWU). In the eyes of many, the ALP's pro-war stance and support for Britain threatened its claim to defend national (as opposed to imperial) patriotism and protect the interests of the labour movement.

As Australian casualties on the battlefields increased, public opinion and Labor's backing for Britain's cause weakened, especially when Billy Hughes succeeded Fisher as Labor leader and prime minister in 1916. Even so, majority opinion was decisively in favour of the war effort. What changed was Hughes's intention to introduce conscription. This brought things to a head, creating the ALP's first split since the disputes in the early years over the caucus pledge and the socialist objective. Once again, Catholic influence on Labor was critical, only this time it exacerbated the division between the pro- and anti-war factions by siding against conscription. One reason was the growing sympathy among Australian Catholics of Irish descent for the 1916 Easter Rising and the cause of Irish self-government, notably following the brutal repression by the British authorities and their execution of the Irish political prisoners after the uprising. Another reason was Catholic opposition to Hughes's perceived or real support for the Protestant ruling class whose pro-conscription policy was supposedly a cover to reverse Australian workers' hard-earned rights. Other factors included isolationist suspicions of empire, the belief that Australia's contribution to "old world troubles" was more than sufficient, resistance to compulsion on grounds of civil liberties, and disappointment with a wartime ALP government that was – or was at least seen to be – on the side of elites and not the people.[34] Even though such pressures were real and disruptive, it was clear that public opinion was pro-war. But the fight over conscription changed everything.

All these reasons reflected noble sentiments, but as Nick Dyrenfurth and Frank Bongiorno observed, "anti-conscriptionism was not unproblematic for Labor either, if considered in terms of the party's established attitude to the relationship between state and citizen. Hitherto a champion of compulsion for the common good, Labor now insisted on the primacy of individual liberty".[35] In other words, the ALP's opposition to conscription moved the party away from its paradoxical disposition of "compulsion for the common good" – duty and obligation to others for the greater good of the nation. In this instance, majority Catholic opinion within Labor supported a more binary choice of an anti-war and anti-conscription policy that made the party look potentially jingoistic and isolationist, not patriotic and internationalist. Inside the party, Hughes's fiercest critic was T. J. Ryan, Labor premier of Queensland (1915-19) and a Catholic lawyer whose widely noticed anti-conscription speech (printed in the Queensland *Hansard*) was almost seized on the orders of the federal government. Brian McKinlay notes that one figure loomed most antagonistic to Hughes' plans:

> Outside the Labor Party Hughes' most impassionate and most effective opponent was Dr Daniel Mannix, who spoke to huge rallies in all the major centres, and whose influence undoubtedly turned much of the Catholic vote against the war. His actions provoked widespread outcry against religious intervention in politics. It also stirred the deep-seated feelings lying beneath the surface of Australian society, and effectively wedded a substantial section of Catholic opinion to the Labor Party, for many years to come.[36]

This realignment was helped by what W. A. Greening called the "Mannix thesis" in Catholic secondary education, namely his mission to push back against the white Anglo-Saxon Protestant ascendancy with its anti-Catholic sectarianism and discrimination by promoting education for Catholics with government support for the running of Catholic schools.[37] To this day, this remains one of the main conduits for diffusing some of the ideas that are central to the social justice tradition of Catholicism in Australia, notably that personal freedom requires social solidarity, that individual rights involve mutual obligations, and that fraternity is interpersonal rather than merely left to individuals in the marketplace or imposed by the collective state.

Here it is instructive to return to the issue of conscription: when Hughes called and lost the referendum on conscription, he was excluded from the Labor Party in his home state of New South Wales on 15 September 1916, after he had walked out of caucus together with 24 fellow members in order to found the National Labor Party, thus splitting both the federal government and the ALP. The resurgence of political-religious sectarianism in Australian politics coincided with the first of two major splits within Labor in the first half of the twentieth century. From the point of view of the ALP's Catholic-inflected radical moderation, this was a disaster as the party became associated with class (and religious) warfare rather than a balance between the labour interest and patriotic duty. Coupled with some trade union support for the Bolshevik revolution and the expulsion in November 1920 from the Australian Parliament of the Irish-born Catholic Labor MP Hugh Mahon for disloyalty to the Empire, the ALP looked increasingly sectarian and extreme. This was not helped by the adoption at the 1921 federal conference of a socialist objective committing the party to "the nationalisation of banking and all principal industries".[38] While this did not amount to the abolition of private property and was meant to be used "for the purpose of preventing exploitation", it ended up tipping the balance in favour of radicalism. Many moderate party members and voters increasingly perceived Labor politics as a form of ideological extremism rather than principled pragmatism – the latter paradox growing out of the influence of Burkean ideas on Labor, which the following chapter explores in greater detail.

Although the severe defeats in elections during the years 1919-1925 were followed by some electoral successes at state level, the ALP entered an era of factional strife that further dented its claim to being a party of national patriotic and democratic renewal. With the first split over conscription not healed, a second split occurred over economic policy in the aftermath of the Great Depression in 1929-32. After James Scullin, a devout Catholic, won a landslide victory in the 1929 elections, the onset of the recession and soaring unemployment in Australia – to levels not seen since the 1890s – led to a showdown between the fiscally conservative wing of the ALP led by Scullin and his treasurer, Joseph Lyons, on the one hand, and the economically radical wing represented by the firebrand leader and premier of New South Wales, Jack Lang, on the other. The Melbourne Agreement and then the Premiers' Plan enshrined fiscal orthodoxy and provoked a backlash that left Labor deeply divided between two increasingly extreme positions – deflation or suspending debt repayments. In turn, this brought about extra-parliamentary paramilitary groups ready to take on Langites in case democracy and social order would break down. Robert Murray has observed that Langism was less about policy and more about a certain "cast of mind . . . a contagion, politically treacherous, intimidating and demagogic, looking to mob oratory as its tool".[39]

Gone was the radical moderation associated with the ALP and the influence of the social justice tradition of the churches. Labor lost not only the December 1931 federal elections, but was also defeated in its New South Wales heartland in state elections in 1932 – both Lang Labor and the anti-Langite federal ALP fighting against each other in separate parties. Similar divisions occurred in Victoria and in South Australia where a three-way split within the Labor Party (Federal Labor, Premiers' Plan Labor and Lang Labor) handed the Liberal and Country League power on a silver tray. Even if the situation seemed more stable in Queensland and Western Australia, the split of 1929-31 over economic policy and the style of politics were in some sense worse than the one over conscription. This was because it cast a long shadow over Labor's paradoxical disposition: its radical moderation was now in doubt as the party seemed to abandon its commitment to a decent and secure life for working people by civilising capitalism and working through the institutions of parliamentary democracy. Labor's soul was once again in question.

After Scullin's loss in 1931, at the national level the ALP was out of power for nearly a decade. In those years, Lyons quit Labor along with James Fenton in anger at Scullin's reinstatement of Ted Theodore (deemed by them as too weak to hold the line against left-wing Lang Labor). Lyons went on to lead the United Australia Party (UAP) and presided over a faster economic recovery than the United States experienced during F. D. Roosevelt's New Deal, which allowed him temporarily to claim the mantle of both fiscal discipline and socio-economic progress.[40] This was natural ALP territory, which the party had abandoned while in power and struggled to recover during its years in opposition until the election of John Curtin as Labor leader in 1935.

Curtin and Labor's post-war settlement

John Curtin embodied Labor's paradoxical disposition in many ways, and his leadership helped to restore the ALP's position as a party of both labour and the national interest. A lifetime in the labour movement as a union and Socialist Party activist in Victoria, an anti-conscription campaigner, and a labour movement newspaper editor in Western Australia, lent Curtin a particular commitment to social welfare, demonstrated from his days of being a member of a Royal Commission on Child Endowment and his attention to the work of the International Labour Organisation in Geneva. His leadership of the party from 1935 onwards focused on restoring unity and re-admitting those ALP members who had quit alongside Lang. But soon the slide into totalitarianism in Europe exposed simmering tensions within the party and the wider labour movement. Events in Germany, Italy, and Spain raised once more the question over whether Labor was isolationist and pacifist or interventionist and ready to engage in military action against the twin threats of Fascism and Communism. The Spanish Civil War and the destruction of democratic government at the hands of Franco emboldened parts of the ALP's left wing and created divisions with right-wing groups that were predominantly Catholic and vehemently opposed what they saw as an attempted Communist conquest of Spain.

Excursus: Curtin and Santamaria

These right-wing groups included a new movement created by B. A. Santamaria with the support of Archbishop Mannix, which in some form or other was active from the late 1930s until the Labor Split in 1954-57 and its aftermath.[41] However, it is wrong to assert that Mannix and Santamaria were unconditional champions of Franco and the fascists in Spain or elsewhere, as some accounts of ALP histories suggest. First of all, Franco was a nationalist military dictator who enjoyed the support of Fascist Italy and Nazi Germany, and the ideology of his regime included semi-fascistic besides monarchist, Catholic, conservative, and other elements. The historian of fascism in Spain, Stanley Payne, argues that "scarcely any of the serious historians and analysts of Franco consider the *generalissimo* to be a core fascist".[42]

Secondly, Santamaria – like Mannix – was always much more anti-Communist and pro-Catholic than openly supportive of Mussolini or Franco. They backed the Vatican and the activities of Catholic Action against the fascist regime in Italy because, for them, the church came first and the state second. It is true that Mannix declared in late 1936 (in a context of increased attacks on Catholics in Republican-controlled areas) that Spain represented a fight between Catholicism and Communism, but in the same year he said that the Franco-led rebels "may be as bad as those they are fighting against".[43] Support for the Catholic Church led Mannix and Santamaria to consider the brutal dictatorship of Franco as a lesser evil compared with the atheist attacks on Catholics by the Communists under the cover of the Republican front.

Third, Santamaria consistently campaigned not just against Communism and Socialism but also against capitalism. A problem, however, was his support for a policy of appeasement vis-à-vis Nazi Germany and Fascist Italy in the false hope that the totalitarian systems would neutralise and perhaps even destroy each other. But Santamaria was hardly unusual. As Robert Murray remarks:

> Labor had also favoured appeasement, as ardently as Santamaria and the Right, though more from a pacifist, isolationist sentiment. While it cannot be seriously argued that Santamaria was ever a fascist, this sort of overriding urgency about communism and a tendency to see the world as facing catastrophe was to characterise much of his career.[44]

For these and other reasons, Santamaria's political outlook was far more complex than a simple embrace of Catholic authoritarianism or outright fascism. His position was based on a critique of the "Whig interpretation of history" and what he called in his memoirs the "philosophic liberalism of the Enlightenment", which found an extension in the materialist ideology of "Marxism with its vision of an earthly paradise this side of the grave, and its categorisation of religion as the opiate of the people".[45] Combined with this critique was a political vision anchored in a Christian-inspired social order. As Santamaria wrote in the first edition of the weekly newspaper, *Catholic Worker*, which he launched in 1936:

> We have come into existence because there is a solution which the

Catholic Church alone can provide, and because there is a taunt to which the Church must reply. The problem which has to be solved is the social problem, a problem of universal importance, affecting every nation and every individual. . . . The new Communism is only the old capitalism plus a little missionary fervour. Both are the illegitimate offspring of the same diseased materialism; both insult Man by regarding him as a labor unit rather than as God's noblest creation; both regulate their behaviour by economic expediency rather than by considerations of justice. Catholicism is the only creed which proclaims the inviolability of the personality of every individual; which proclaims that every individual must be in receipt of sufficient means to be free from that perpetual anxiety concerning his livelihood, which distracts his mind from primary things. . .[46]

The idea of justice conceptualised as the dignity of the person and the commitment to secure freedom from want and from fear resonated strongly with large sections of the labour movement and the ALP, in particular the Catholic community at its heart.

Whatever his many flaws, Santamaria maintained a consistency in his thinking that can best be understood in paradoxical terms as economically egalitarian and socially conservative. In 1941, for example, he penned the lead article of the first issue of *Freedom*, the Movement's weekly publication, in which he defined the vision in terms of the

need for a fighting paper devoted without reserve to the cause of social reconstruction based on the inspiration of Christianity, the desire for justice among all classes, and the militant defence of freedom – menaced today by the external enemy and the cruel fanatics, of both the Right and the Left, who seek to destroy our democracy and submerge it in the brutality of Fascism or of Communism. . . . The root trouble is not economic. Certainly we must have a REAL family wage, marriage loans, increased baby bonuses, proper houses (owned by the worker) and great economic security. But the causes of our population decline are as much moral and social as economic.[47]

What is striking about this statement is not just the rejection of Fascism and of Communism in equal terms as brutal systems but also the argument that politics needed to marry economics with culture if it is to build a social order based on a substantive conception of justice. This conception and Santamaria's political thought more widely were decisively influenced by Catholic social teaching and its search for constructive alternatives to capitalist individualism and communist collectivism. After all, Santamaria was the main drafting author of the annual Social Justice Statement issued by the Australian Catholic bishops in the years from 1941 until 1957.

Here was great overlap and convergence with the ALP and its ethical outlook. Indeed, as Gerard Henderson reports, Santamaria wrote in his memoirs "that the Victorian State Labor MP Bert Cremean 'originally proposed the idea that the Catholic bishops should themselves produce, or officially endorse, an annual statement, which would seek to apply the social principles of Christianity to a particular national social problem'".[48] Among the themes running through the statements were calls for a "family wage" – "a man's earning shall be sufficient to meet the requirements of the family", workers owning property as well as child and other benefits supporting families for all social classes. The social justice statements struck a chord with many ALP politicians, including Curtin, who, as prime minister, wrote in a letter to Santamaria on 25 May 1941 that the principles set out in *Justice Now!* constitute "an excellent basis for discussion for a better social order". At the same time, he pointed out that "many of the ideals contained therein are set out in Labor's platform and have been referred to by myself in policy speeches".[49]

Part of the reason why Catholic social teaching and Labor principles converged is because both promoted an understanding of justice aimed at reconciling estranged interests, above all capital and labour, in a negotiated settlement based on the dignity of the person, the rule of law, and parliamentary democracy. As the tide turned from the threat of invasion to the prospect of victory in early 1943, Labor and the Catholic Church shifted their attention to the task of post-war reconstruction. In addition to submitting an eighty-page pamphlet entitled, "Statement on Reconstruction: Pattern for Peace", which he had written together with a committee of Catholics, Santamaria also launched an ecumenical initiative on a new economic and social settlement. A joint committee consisting of Catholics, Anglicans, and the other Protestant churches (Baptist, Congregational, Methodist, and Presbyterian) developed a *Christian Programme for Social Justice* with twenty points, among them:

- the public control of monopolies and credit;

- the creation of Industrial Councils, which are self-governing bodies representing employers, employees, and the public and in charge of setting wages, prices, dividends and profits;

- help for small owners;

- worker co-ownership of industry;

- the extension of the cooperative movement, including in the rural economy and communities;

- the recognition of the principle of adequate income for all, including those on the land;

- special assistance to family life, including a marriage bonus, adequate family allowances, child endowment;

- adequate wages before profits and dividends;

- equal pay for equal work;

- family homes for those in need;

- decentralisation;

- revision of farming policy so that the first principle of farming is to provide for the subsistence of the farmer and his family;

- fair returns for farm products and the creation of a self-governing body to direct agricultural development;

- a national system of education;

- religion as the basis of education.

Then as now, the last point is particularly controversial but, as the 1943 and 1944 Social Justice Statements made clear, while the state has an indispensable role to play in relation to industrial policy, farming, credit policy, and wages, the content of education should be as free as possible from political interference:

> We have already seen in Germany and other countries that, if you hand over to the State the complete training of youth, you inevitably produce a generation that blindly obeys dictators and can easily be filled with any non-sense about race-superiority. . . . The world suffers intensely from excessive nationalism . . . to deprive our school system of variety and of the inspiration of the Christian religion as an essential element in education would be to make straight the way of the despot.[50]

The ALP led by Curtin might not have signed up to every one of the twenty points, but Curtin's vision for both national defence and a post-war settlement overlapped significantly with some of the key elements in the social justice programme.

Curtin's leadership

Curtin was able to resolve the tensions within the ALP between the secular left and the Catholic right over foreign policy because of one crucial factor: the threat of Japanese invasion. Nothing concentrates the mind more than enslavement by a foreign power. Curtin managed to steer a 'radically moderate' course on how to prepare Australia for the prospect of war and its aftermath. Against the Lyons-led government and its reluctance to undertake a programme of increased military expenditure, Curtin persuaded a majority in his party to commit to boosting expenditure on the country's air defences. This neutralised Labor's potential weakness on national security and avoided re-opening the old wounds over conscription. Curtin combined some important electoral victories in 1937 with a staunch anti-Communist stance when the ALP rejected the offer by the Communist Party of Australia for a single popular resistance against fascism, arguing instead that "it is by membership of the ALP alone that a united front can be presented by the workers of the Commonwealth against the forces of war, fascism and reaction generally".[51] This is how Curtin sought to reconcile the labour interest with the national interest and the party's internationalism with Australian patriotism.

On becoming Prime Minister in 1941, he declared: "We [the Labor government] regard the war as one which affects the basic interests of Labor more than those of any other section of the community".[52] A lapsed Catholic, Curtin worked closely with Ben Chifley, himself of Irish Catholic descent though married with Presbyterian rites, and the government they led together largely reflected the ethos of the churches' social justice tradition that is economically radical and socially moderate. Among other things, both Curtin and Chifley were born into humble circumstances and their rise to the highest office in the land owed a lot to the meritocratic ethos that animated Labor – combined with an understanding of how inequalities of power, wealth, and social status blight people's everyday existence.

As part of defence planning, the Curtin government made the fight against unemployment its key domestic priority by expanding the war industries to provide jobs to those who had suffered for so long in the wake of the Great Depression, especially in strategically important sectors such as aircraft and shipbuilding. Full employment was achieved for the first time in the history of independent Australia, and the worst of poverty was eliminated by 1942. All this helped to boost national cohesion at a time when, due to the war effort, the governing Labor Party had to bring in rationing of petrol, food, and clothes. This was counterbalanced by strict price controls and heavy taxes on high incomes and corporate profits in order to minimise profiteering. Together with Chifley, Curtin introduced a national system of widows' pensions and he increased Commonwealth funding for public health, children, and the disabled. Greater economic justice and social stability were the hallmarks of the Labor wartime government. This laid the foundations for a new post-war settlement which shaped decisively both the party and the country – notably the powers of the Commonwealth in the areas of taxation and social welfare.

Having led the campaign against conscription in 1916, Curtin was careful to avoid a repeat not just by relying on voluntary recruitment. Following the bombing of Pearl Harbour on 7 December 1941, and the encroaching advance of Japanese forces in Asia and the Pacific, Curtin acted quickly by repatriating Australia's only battle-seasoned force stationed in the Middle East. Darwin was bombed by Japanese aircraft in 1942. With the support of his cabinet, Curtin took a strong stance in favour of the national interest. Although it could be argued that the Australian political establishment were entirely complacent in the 1930s and neglectful of preparing for the nation's defence, the governments mostly in power that decade bore most of the opprobrium. The failure by the Lyons and the Menzies governments to prepare the country's air power left major cities defenceless. Moreover, the Labor government stood up to Winston Churchill on three key questions: first, seeking American support "free of any pangs as to our traditional links or kinship with the United Kingdom"; second, insisting that Singapore should not be evacuated by the British in the face of Japanese aggression; third, refusing to let Australian troops that were returning home from the Middle East be diverted to Burma in order to assist Britain. At the same time, Curtin's close ties, forged in wartime, with the United States, notably with General MacArthur who became the Supreme Commander of Allies Forces in the South-West Pacific, exposed Curtin to criticisms of compromising Australian sovereignty. He sought to hold the balance by positioning the country as one of the pillars of the liberal West against fascism.

Crucially, Curtin maintained party unity by moving Labor back to a position of radical moderation. Faced with the existential threat from Japanese militarism, Curtin persuaded the ALP to accept that conscripts be sent abroad to fight the troops of the Japanese Emperor. This could be reasonably argued as 'self-defence' rather than fighting someone else's war. Curtin's position was endorsed by a decision at a special Labor conference. Curtin and nearly all ministers (Calwell being a notable dissenter) thereby prevented a repeat of the split in 1916. Curtin's new-found pragmatism earned him admiration and affection across the party and the country. As Nick Dyrenfurth and Frank Bongiorno note:

> The Great War anti-conscriptionist now found himself at the head of
> a wartime government practising conscription; the socialist apprentice
> of Frank Anstey was promising not to use the war to pursue the
> nationalisation of industry. Meanwhile, the internationalism learned at
> Tom Mann's feet had given way to Australian nationalism and British
> race patriotism.[53]

Curtin's radically reforming government and its attempt to shift
power from the states to the federal level did however run into the
opposition of the High Court and certain sectional interests. A
referendum in 1944 to transfer constitutional powers to the federal
government was lost. Paradoxically, this forced Labor to expand, in
its post-war vision, on the significance of states. The party's approach
of moderately progressive reforms animated ALP state governments
throughout the 1940s.

As soon as Labor departed from this course, it tended to lose
power both at federal and at a state level. In the late 1940s it was still
reaping a peace dividend. The effects of complacency set in. After
Curtin's sudden death in July 1945, Chifley succeeded him. Initially the
new prime minister entrenched the post-war settlement by combining
Labor's commitment to a social market in pursuit of economic justice
with an active state that could help to foster social stability. This was
expressed most clearly by the ambition to bring about, and maintain,
full employment. In this manner, Chifley's government stayed true to
Labor's ambition of being a national popular party that represents both
the interest of the country and that of the wider labour movement.
In relation to immigration and foreign policy, the priority was to hold
in balance Australia's role within the wider Western alliance and its
particular location in the Indo-Pacific region. That is why Chifley

sought to consolidate cooperation with the United States and expand ties with the new and emerging independent nations of Asia while also remaining an integral part of the British Commonwealth. Arthur Calwell who formulated the new post-war immigration policy fused the old Labor allegiance to White Australia with a new opening towards European migrants that would change the demographic composition of the country forever. He and Chifley justified this in terms of the ALP's claim to be the party of nation-building in which the labour interest is fully represented through much-expanded opportunities for education and employment.

Despite a much smaller majority in the 1946 elections, Chifley and his government failed to learn the lessons of the earlier radicalisation and the ensuing splits, especially over Lang's economic policy. Chifley's decision in August 1947 to ambush his cabinet with an ill-considered proposal to nationalise the banks ran into concerted opposition from the conservative-dominated Liberal Party under Menzies. The latter, now opposition leader, exploited the turmoil to mobilise public opinion against Labor. When the High Court ruled that the nationalisation of banks was unconstitutional, 'Chif' soldiered on promising to pursue his policy by referendum if need be. In the confusion, the private bank employee associations were foremost in leading opposition to the Labor government. Public hostility defeated Labor and this plan in the 1949 elections. The coalition behind the ALP's wartime and post-war unity began to disintegrate. Chifley also lost the April 1951 elections and died in June that year. Labor under his successor Dr H. V. ('Doc') Evatt descended into internal strife between two rival factions: one close to the Communists and their fellow travellers and the other associated with Catholic Action and the Movement led by Santamaria.

Evatt had already incurred the wrath of some of the party's right faction over his contribution in defeating the proposed constitutional ban of the Communist Party of Australia (CPA) in a referendum in 1951 and his role as legal counsel for the CPA-controlled Waterside Workers' Federation in a challenge to the Act earlier in the High Court prior to the referendum. Combined with vicious attacks from Menzies's Liberal Party, Evatt's failure to hold the line in the clash between Labor's two militant factions led to the third split and the creation of the break-away Democratic Labor Party (DLP), which kept Labor out of power for a generation and permanently deepened the division between the more progressive and the more small-c conservative strands. Inside the ALP and the wider labour movement, the social justice tradition of the churches lacked leadership to mediate among these factions. As a result, social Catholicism became increasingly subsumed under ideological categories of left versus right, with significant differences between the States, reflecting the nature of the ALP Split – NSW largely holding together; Victoria and Queensland losing significant support to the breakaway DLP.

Evatt, Calwell and the legacy of the double Split

Australia in the early 1950s was in the grip of growing ideological divisions. This was especially so between the forces of conservatism represented by the Liberal Party under Menzies and large parts of the press and the forces sympathetic to Communism in some trade unions and elements of the ALP. One reason for the political instability is that the post-war settlement proved insufficiently robust to address the needs and interests of many working Australians. As the euphoria of the immediate post-1945 period faded, the rising tensions of the

Cold War overshadowed the growing unease among the working class in the face of changing social conditions, including higher inflation and an insufficient improvement in living standards after years of sacrifice. In turn, this favoured the influence of the CPA in parts of the trade unions and among some ALP members. In some instances, the Communist infiltration of trade unions was shifting the balance within the labour movement away from the radically moderate middle towards ideological extremism.

Meanwhile, certain Catholics in the wider labour movement tried to realign the party with its right wing and some of them organised themselves in the form of the Industrial Groups. These were coordinated by a secretive organisation – the Movement, originally called the Catholic Social Studies Movement marshalled by Santamaria and supported by the Australian bishops. With the support of Archbishop Mannix, the Movement intended to wrest control of the ALP from what it viewed as a Communist coup within the trade unions and by extension the party.[54] But success created hubris. By 1953 the communists were well and truly on the run in the unions. They had lost the Ironworkers, the Clerks', most of the branches of the rail unions, and the coast seemed clear to emasculate their influence entirely. But then personality politics combined with factional antagonisms created the biggest ALP split of them all.

As the Split broke out in Victoria, Evatt and his supporters were accused of being agents of Communism, while the Industrial Groups were viewed as a front for Santamaria's right-wing brand of Catholicism. The clash involved Evatt attacking what he called "a small minority group of Labor members located particularly in Victoria, which has since 1949 become increasingly disloyal to the Labor movement and to the Labor leadership". Deciding to take on the Movement without offering any proof of disloyalty to Labor, Evatt went on to allege that "it seems certain that the activities of this small group are largely directed from outside the Labor movement. The Melbourne *News-Weekly* [Santamaria's co-edited publication previously named *Freedom*] appears as their organ. A serious position exists".[55] These were inflammatory claims.

The double effect of Evatt's explosive intervention was to bring Labor Party internal enmities into the open and highlight tensions within the Catholic Church over whether the ultimate authority was with the lay national executive of the Movement (headed by Santamaria), the bishops who formally oversaw the Catholic Social Studies Movement, or the (arch)bishop in each diocese in which the Movement operated. Just as the Labor Party ended up splitting both in Victoria and at the federal level with the establishment of the breakaway DLP, so too the church split over whether to support Santamaria's leadership of the Movement or take it over (as in Sydney under Bishop Carroll who had the full backing of Cardinal Gilroy). When the ecclesiastical rift reached the Vatican, the ultimate decision sought to keep the clergy out of the political contest and leave the laity in charge of domestic political issues, including pushing back against communism. The Vatican re-stated the Catholic Church's position against creating a "confessional political party" or a lay group such as the Movement taking a "political character upon itself". Instead, the instruction was for lay Catholics to get involved in "the battle against communism" not through "direct action upon unions and political parties" but instead by focusing on the "formation of the social and moral conscience of families" and "to act with determination as individual citizens, within trade unions and political bodies".[56] In fact, both engagement at the personal level (improving oneself) and within unions and the ALP were needed for transformative success.

The problem was that both sides in the Catholic split went against the spirit of the Vatican decision. Santamaria's newly established Catholic Social Movement supported the DLP against the ALP, just as Bishop Carroll used the renamed Episcopal Commission on the Catholic Social Studies Movement in Sydney to oppose the DLP and support candidates within the trade unions aligned with the ALP. Gerard Henderson makes the point that twenty years after the events of 1954-57, Santamaria said that "he had been accused of dividing the Church, but stated defiantly that, in his view, it was better for the Church to be divided and half right than to be united and totally wrong. All very Santamaria, to be sure".[57] As the Church and the ALP splintered, Santamaria was one of the hotheads.

There can be little doubt that up until the split with the DLP, Santamaria's ambition was to influence the ALP in the direction of his political agenda based on Catholic social teaching, as he saw it. In a letter to Mannix at the end of 1952, he set out his programme in somewhat hyperbolic terms:

> Within a period of five or six years, the [Catholic] Social Studies Movement should be able to completely transform the leadership of the Labor Movement and introduce into Federal and States spheres large numbers of members who possess a clear realisation of what Australia demands of them and the will to carry it out. . . . They should be able to implement a Christian social programme. . . . This is the first time that such a work has become possible in Australia, and as far as I can see in the Anglo-Saxon world since the advent of Protestantism.[58]

Santamaria's strategy involved working with Catholic Labor politicians like Bert Cremean in Victoria and James ('Jim') Kenny in NSW, as well as non-Catholic union and ALP figures, including Percy Clarey, James Victor Stout, Reg Broadby and Denis ('Dinny') Lovegrove in Victoria. But a version of the 1952 letter to Mannix became public during the Split and caused a massive backlash, fuelled by long-standing suspicions that Santamaria's Movement was a coordinated authoritarian Catholic intervention in politics. This, the claim went, vindicated the left's hostility and mobilised liberal Protestants. Interestingly, Santamaria's overt, 'muscular Catholic' pushiness alienated moderate union leaders and others, right up to the New South Wales premier, Joe Cahill.

Before the splits in the mid-1950s, for Santamaria, the double danger was the attempted Communist control of the trade unions and the rise of a new force, Bevanism (named after the British Labour politician, Aneurin Bevan), which could tilt the balance within the ALP towards state socialism, anti-imperialism, and proto-communism. Evatt's attack on the Movement exacerbated the deepening divisions within the ALP.[59] Communism was largely in check by 1953. But 'Bevanism' – a tendency that Santamaria exaggerated – was an inchoate force. In Santamaria's mind soft-headed Fabianism and anti-American, isolationist thinking loomed as the new enemy. As Michael Easson, the former Secretary of the New South Wales Labor Council, has written, "Evatt's leadership not only contributed to the final tragedy but also initiated and worsened the disaster".[60]

Indeed, Evatt's actions contributed to the resurgence of anti-Catholic sectarianism that had never dominated the party but equally had never gone away. The spectre of sectarian politics returned to Australia and it opened a deep and ultimately unbridgeable split within the ALP that would keep the party out of office between

1949 and 1972, as first Evatt and then Calwell each lost three elections in a row. The double split – within the ALP and the Catholic Church – prevented the Labor Party from transforming the country and undercut the influence of Catholic social teaching in Australian politics. Yet, at the same time, social Catholicism helped to prevent a Communist take-over of the labour movement and kept the ALP more moderate by tempering the rise of the secular, radical left. It remained a source of reconciliation that could build bridges and once more bring the party together. In fact, Calwell himself was a good example, as he prepared the ground for a fundamental shift away from Anglo-Celtic immigration, writing to Chifley to declare his "determination to develop a heterogeneous society: a society where Irishness and Roman Catholicism would be as acceptable as Englishness and Protestantism: where an Italian background would be as acceptable as a Greek, a Dutch or any other".[61] Calwell still felt uncomfortable, however, with Asian immigration. In Labor ranks, he was one of the last proponents of the of White Australia sentiment.

Like other Catholics in the ALP, Calwell was a staunch anti-Communist who, in 1950, wrote about his long battle and that of the party against Communism, quoting Pius XI's phrase that "The great scandal of the nineteenth century was that the workers of the world were lost to Christ". One year earlier, Calwell had published a tract entitled, "What the Popes Have Said on Capitalism, the Employing Class and Trade Unions".[62] His text draws on the social encyclicals and the *Catholic Worker* as well as statements by Archbishop Mannix and some French cardinals in order to underline Catholic opposition to monopoly capitalism. "This is not a propaganda pamphlet", writes Calwell, "but it is an attempt to put the record straight for those who are interested in the future of this great nation and who want to see our social order founded on Christian principles".[63] Calwell was well-read in Catholic polemics and personally scandalised by Movement claims that he was soft on communist influence on the ALP.

As for Santamaria, his attempt to promote his particular agenda was doomed from the moment the moderate right wing of the ALP stayed in the party and did not go with the breakaway DLP. He was certainly consistent in his opposition to the Communists and their fellow travellers in the labour movement, but for reasons of ideological purity he poured scorn on all those in the ALP who pursued a strategy of stay-in-and-fight, notably the moderate Labor right in New South Wales around Bill Coulbourne, the NSW ALP General-Secretary, and activists such as Matt Keating, father of Paul Keating. It was not until the latter's rise that elements of Catholic social teaching and the justice tradition of the churches would become once again more influential within the ALP.

Whitlam and Labor's return to radical moderation

In the years between the ALP Split and the rise of Gough Whitlam as party leader (from 1967), the ALP was divided at the federal and state level, especially in Victoria and also in Queensland but much less so in New South Wales, where Joe Cahill, a Catholic, ensured that there was no direct clash between the ALP and the Catholic Church. The same was true in Tasmania where the Labor government survived despite some electoral gains for the DLP. More generally, Labor lacked leadership to heal the rift that had given rise to the DLP split. Evatt did not have the character or vision to seek reconciliation, while Santamaria and Mannix continued to be more worried about Communism than about advancing Catholic ideas via a reunited Labor Party. Calwell reversed Labor's electoral losses of 1955 and 1958 and nearly won the 1961 election, but a combination of foreign policy disagreements and Menzies's decision to grant state aid to private schools ensured that the Liberal Party easily won the snap election in 1963 in part thanks to Catholic votes through the preference-support of the DLP. While the ALP was successful in attracting some more middle-class voters, it could not win without its Catholic working-class base. Indeed, before the split, two-thirds of Catholics voted Labor. The realignment after 1954-57 saw parts of the Catholic community switch their direct or preference-support from Labor to the Liberals, which denied the ALP a majority.

From 1949 until the Hawke-Keating governments in 1983-96, the ALP only once held power nationally for three years when Gough Whitlam was elected Prime Minister in 1972 and ended up being dismissed from office by the Governor-General in 1975. Whitlam overhauled almost all of the ALP's policies during his time in opposition. Under his leadership, the ALP once more became a force of national renewal. Both in opposition and in government, Whitlam focused on an ambitious domestic reform programme that spanned health, transport, housing, urban planning, and above all education. Part of Whitlam's success was in building an electoral coalition between the working class who were more socially conservative and lived in suburban or regional communities, on the one hand, and a more disparate electorate made up of students, teachers, people in the arts and media, as well as other groups who were progressive and lived in urban areas, on the other. Using a disarmingly simple election slogan, "It's Time", Whitlam promised to lead a government with

three aims: They are – to promote equality, to involve the people of

Australia in the decision-making process, and to liberate the talents
and uplift the horizons of the Australian people. We want to give a
new life, and a new meaning in this new nation, to the touchstone of
modern democracy – to liberty, equality, fraternity.[64]

Key to Whitlam's electoral success and his legacy for the labour
movement were reforms of party organisation that preceded his
election in 1972. In the late 1960s, the ALP belatedly dealt with the
divisions in Victoria and, to a lesser extent, in New South Wales. The
Victorian Right and Centre, or what remained after the Split, was
quarantined to ineffectual minority status. With Whitlam's support
those elements, though not the DLP officials and activists, were finally
brought back in after their exile in the late 1950s and throughout the
1960s. Conversely, the NSW Left was given greater representation
than had been the case previously. Taken together, these changes
satisfied many across the two factions of the party and brought
about the reconciliation that had eluded both Evatt and Calwell. As
Dyrenfurth and Bongiorno argue:

> Intervention [in favour of the Right and the Centre] outraged much
> of the Victorian Left, but it laid the foundations for Labor's federal
> revival. In fact it did much more than that: it also created the basis of
> the modern Labor Party. The early 1970s reorganisation in Victoria
> and New South Wales destroyed the party's winner-take-all culture and
> was an essential precondition for the nationally organised factions that
> later emerged. . . . But there would also be a price to pay if factions
> degenerated into mere instruments for the distribution of party spoils
> [as would be the case in particular during the Rudd-Gillard-Rudd years].[65]

Moreover, Whitlam strengthened the representation of
parliamentarians on both the Federal Executive and Federal
Conference which was henceforth open to the public. Connected to
party reform was a fundamental overhaul of Labor's policies, including

two particularly controversial issues: non-white immigration and state aid for Catholic schools, which was especially sensitive given the split with the DLP and the fact that the post-war baby and immigration boom crowded Catholic schools. Whitlam presented these reforms as progressive and forward-looking, which enhanced Labor's growing appeal to a more middle-class electorate who worked in liberal professions and were socially progressive. At the same time, he maintained the support of the ALP's working-class blue-collar voters and even regained the trust of some Catholics who had stopped voting Labor after the split and who were more socially conservative.

Whitlam's preference for progressive modernisation, however, over the small-c conservative outlook set in train an evolution that ended up with the ascendancy of a university-educated professional class that made it increasingly difficult for manual workers to rise up through the ranks of the trade unions and all the way to federal parliament. Henceforth, there was a danger that the ALP would sacrifice the labour interest on the altar of electoral success in ways that jeopardised its original working-class soul. This danger would beset the governments led by the four Labor prime ministers who have defined the direction of the party in the present day – Hawke, Keating, Rudd, and Gillard.

In short, with Whitlam, Labor entered a new age defined by the profound cultural changes of the 1960s and 1970s. From its origins in the labour movement in the 1850s to losing power in 1975, the party changed beyond recognition. Yet at the same time, it remained the same – an expression of both the labour interest and the national interest. This expression is always dynamic and never static. In the meantime, the various splits in the ALP brought about a fundamental realignment towards the party's Left and Right factions.

This realignment mirrored the shift away from the old religious-political sectarianism in the direction of a newer opposition between liberal-progressive and conservative-communitarian values in the two main parties and in the Catholic Church following the reforms of the Second Vatican Council. These shifts raise questions about the philosophical ideas and ethical traditions underpinning Australian Labor. Before exploring the ALP's contemporary moral purpose, it is instructive to consider the governing philosophy that right from its inception made Labor such a unique party.

3

Philosophy
Labor's traditions and
dispositions

The ALP's philosophical roots

What is Australian Labor for? What is its moral and civic vision for the country? From the party's creation until now, it sought to represent both the labour interest and the national interest, giving people a share in power and prosperity and enabling them to partake of the good life, as chapters 1 and 2 suggest. This argument raises questions about the intellectual traditions and cultural dispositions that underpin Labor's ethical purpose. The present chapter explores some of the deep philosophical beliefs and values that have shaped the Australian labour movement and given the ALP its distinct identity. Labor does not have a single fixed essence but a series of governing principles that partially overlap and criss-cross – a constellation perhaps best captured by the philosopher Ludwig Wittgenstein's notion of 'family resemblances'.[1]

This is rather more precise than the cliché about the party being a broad church. It is often said about the British Labour Party that it owes more to Methodism than to Marxism. The ALP comprises different strands that encompass elements of those traditions and much in between them. While egalitarianism and small-l liberalism have been present in the ALP for all of its history, Burkean thematics and Catholic personalism are just as important for understanding the party's ethical outlook. This can be summarised as a commitment to economic justice and social stability that creates the conditions for people to pursue the common good; a life in which individuals can find fulfilment through mutual flourishing in relations with others.

Why might this matter? Politics is not primarily about policies. It is not even predominantly about personalities and their political platforms. Rather, the lifeblood of a democratic polity is a contest of ideas between the main parties and within themselves. Such contests force attention on the nature of society and the pre-political 'we' on which a common life depends – the bonds binding together neighbourhoods and nations. Parties need programmes and policies but they also require an underlying philosophy and an animating purpose which provide a moral compass to navigate the tough and often brutal arena of politics.

It might be argued, however, that this is too idealistic and naïve a characterisation. The generalisation founders on experience. As much as Tony Judt and others want politics to be a contest of ideas, it might be that what the electorate wants is more – more of everything and less hassle to get it. No one would want the common good to be represented in those terms, but is the political programme saleable to the electorate in any other terms? At the 2019 election, Labor promised many of its supporters more, but the way of giving them more was by giving less to others. That was a hard message to sell to an electorate looking for more and untroubled by ideas. Here is where the grinding electoral challenges and policy-making are joined.

The answer is not to dismiss the importance of ideas but to link them to political action. Leadership involves both universal principles and particular situations, and a politics that is both national and popular requires social virtues such as fairness, empathy, honesty, trustworthiness, and loyalty without which it is impossible to build trust, relationships, and coalitions around shared interests. The political right has historically had a broad appeal by calibrating itself to multiple, often contradictory, constituencies – from more traditional and patriotic big-C Conservatives to modernising economic liberals, from more inward-looking nationalists to globalist libertarians. The conservative tradition may be sceptical about utopian visions and grand ideology, but along with the rest of the right, it rarely had a shortage of ideas or thinkers – even though the contemporary disarray of conservatism might suggest otherwise.[2]

By contrast, to paraphrase Judt, the left has tended to be a practice in lifelong search of a theory.[3] The lineage of classical liberalism includes John Locke and J. S. Mill, while the tradition of conservatism claims Edmund Burke, communism Karl Marx, and modern libertarianism Ayn Rand. By contrast, non-Marxist socialism and social democracy lack a seminal political philosopher or group of thinkers. Partly, this is because the left grew out of a reaction against the right in the wake of the French Revolution, often being clearer about what they stood against than what they were for. This stance is still a tendency today when it comes to austerity, national identity, borders, and other salient political as well as public policy issues. Partly, the left lacks a distinctive political philosophy because it is less an ideology than it is a creed, ever evolving and as pragmatic as it is principled.

Arguably, the ALP is one of the earliest expressions of democratic socialism as distinct from Marxist-Leninist communism and small-l liberalism. It is, to quote the words of Albert Métin, an example of "socialism without doctrine".[4] Its intellectual origins lie in the space opened up between conservatism and liberalism by the labour movement and other influential traditions such as English chartists and thinkers such as the distributist Henry George and Edward Bellamy. Over time, democratic socialism evolved into social democracy. The ALP's principles and dispositions are paradoxically as progressive as they are traditional; as radical as they are small-c conservative. Binding these paradoxes together is a certain conception of justice in terms of the common good, which has its roots in the tradition of Catholic social teaching and cognate traditions in Protestantism, guild socialism and the 'new liberalism' of T. H. Green, L. T. Hobhouse and J. A. Hobson.

'Social democracy with Australian characteristics': Labor's ethical socialism

In its history since 1891, ALP electoral successes and political victories more often than not were followed by defeats, disillusionment, and divides within the labour movement. This has kept the party out of power for much of its federal existence. In the eighty-two years between the creation of Labor and the election of the Hawke government, the ALP held office for a mere nineteen of them. Yet Labor obtained its unity and drive to change social conditions for workers and the people as a whole from a governing philosophy that can be described as democratic socialism. This, as Nick Dyrenfurth argues, has coexisted "with populist and radical liberal beliefs, while trade union ideology cohabited with protectionist nationalism (at once economic in terms of supporting high tariffs and racially exclusivist in its attitude to immigration)".[5] Such a variety of values and positions suggests that the ALP lacks a unitary core or essence. Rather, it is a case of 'family resemblances', starting with the commitment to socialism and democracy, which is expressed in the party's objective as defined by its constitution: "The Australian Labor Party is a democratic socialist party and has the objective of the democratic socialisation of industry, production, distribution and exchange, to the extent necessary to eliminate exploitation and other anti-social features in these fields". This end, combined with the means as laid out in the party's Principles of Action, has almost always stood at odds with Labor governments at federal or state level, which nationalised few industries and protected private property.

This does not mean, however, that the ALP in power betrays its stated purpose or that its philosophy is not one of democratic socialism. Rather, it requires a step back to first principles and the realisation that Labor is most of all a practice rather than a theory (Judt's point) and a way of life embodied in relationships and institutions rather than an ideology based on abstraction. The party's practice and way of life grew out of the labour movement, and there is little doubt that it was shaped by socialist ideals that were reflections on the everyday experience of workers – dispossession, powerlessness, and the relentless commodification of labour, land, and life. Already in the 1850s, the ideas of English Chartism helped to strengthen the emerging movement of democratic self-government that would in time transform the penal colony into a self-governing country within the British Commonwealth of Nations. For example, James Stephens (1821-1889) – the founder of Australia's eight-hour day movement – was a Chartist and trade unionist from Wales who together with James Galloway restarted the Operative Masons Society based on Chartist ideas that inspired the creation of the eight-hour day in 1856.

When liberalism became increasingly associated with the oligarchy of free-trade capitalism in the late-nineteenth century, the labour movement turned to radical thinkers such as Henry George whose ideas on land reform were popularised by Australians through newspaper reprints of his book *Progress and Poverty* as well as local groups. One such Australian was Patrick McMahon Glynn, a founding father of the Australian Constitution, who promoted George's approach to land ownership.[6] There were book clubs across the country discussing Edward Bellamy's work, *Looking Backward*, a utopian novel informed by an ethical socialism which advocated consumers' cooperative, an equal amount of credit for all citizens and fewer working hours for those doing dangerous and unpleasant jobs. In an essay on Labor's philosophy, Lloyd Ross writes: "Also widely read were [Laurence] Gronlund's *Cooperative Commonwealth* [1884], [Ignatius Donnelly's] *Caesar's Column* [1891], William Morris' *Dream of John Ball* [1888] and *News from Nowhere* [1890], Olive Schreiner's *Story of an African Farm* [1883], collections of John Stuart Mill's essays. William Lane converted these ideas into an Australian collectivism in his *Workingman's Paradise* [1892]".[7] There were many tributaries that fed into Labor's formation.

What this shows is how Australians translated socialist ideals into a language that was accessible to people across the country, using iconography and popular meaning, as in the poetry and short stories by Henry Lawson – notably *While the Billy Boils* with its deeply realistic description of Australian life as it then was, including the bleakness and loneliness of the Australian bush. Another stark example was Lane's famous definition of socialism as "a desire to be mates" – one of the earliest expressions of Australia's "secular egalitarian creed".[8] This creed was primarily grounded in the lived experiences of workers but it also gave rise to theorisations of democratic socialism. In fact, there was a double movement within the first trade unions and other forms of worker mobilisation. Just as socialism, in a variety of forms, became more popular among the intellectuals and leaders, so too the use of abstract concepts and theoretical language limited the appeal to workers and ordinary people.

Therefore, the labour intelligentsia drew on the popular socialism of Bellamy, Lane, and Lawson. For instance, when asked by the Royal Commission investigating the strikes in 1890 about whether a belief in socialism is widely shared by trade unionists, the leader of the Australian Workers' Union, William Guthrie Spence responded:

> Very widely; more especially in New South Wales and Queensland. In fact generally there is a widespread feeling in favour of some sort of socialism, but men differ as to what it should be. . . . There is a great deal of literature of socialism read, especially in the back

country . . . and it is evolving a desire for change. There is a certain amount of vagueness was to what should be the first practical step. . . . I have no hesitation in saying that there is nothing like a revolutionary feeling in any part of Australia.[9]

However overstated the last sentence may be, it is no exaggeration that the early labour movement was against revolutionary socialism, never mind totalitarian communism, and in favour of a form of popular and parliamentary socialism. The Labor Prime Minister Andrew Fisher put this perhaps best when he said: "No party worthy of the name can deny that its objective is socialism, but no socialist with any parliamentary experience can hope to get anything for many years to come, other than practical legislation of a socialist nature".[10]

That was the meaning of labourism.[11] It shaped Labor's political and ethical outlook decisively from the 1920s to 1950s in the battle against repeated attempts by Communists to take over the unions and the party. The commitment to democratic norms and the sovereignty of parliament was also reflected in the actions of radical reforming governments, from the foundations Fisher laid for building a welfare state, to Scullin's action against economic depression; from Curtin's and Chifley's post-war settlement, to Whitlam's progressive policies. Some of the most notable achievements of the ALP were driven by what Tim Battin rightly describes as "the most sustaining, energising and characteristic of all intellectual traditions in the ALP in recent decades, namely the socialist tradition".[12] This includes welfare benefits such as pensions, unemployment aid, sickness pay, and child allowances, the creation of the Commonwealth Bank of Australia and the Commonwealth Employment Service, fair bargaining arrangements and the provision of apprenticeship, public enterprises, and many more achievements. These reforms were often instigated by the trade unions that rejected both capitalism and communism in favour of a much more mixed market economy based on collective action by workers, many of whom saw themselves as socialist.[13]

Marxist scholars contend that the ALP's governing philosophy is incompatible with socialism on three grounds.[14] First of all, the institutions and processes of bourgeois liberal democracy rule out a socialist agenda. Secondly, capitalism controls both the economy and politics in such a way as to make fundamental reform impossible, short of overthrowing the capitalist system altogether. Thirdly, Marxists claim that the ALP aspires to little more than a bourgeois way of life that keeps workers quiet without rocking the boat. As Humphrey McQueen wrote: "The Labor Party cannot produce socialism because it is part of a class that is fundamentally committed to capitalism".[15] However, this line of argument is flatly contradicted by Labor's fusion of democratic socialist ideals with radical reform that have civilised capitalism. 'Really existing' parliamentary socialism transformed the capitalist logic of dispossessing workers and commodifying labour, land, and life.

Then there are those who argue that the Hawke-Keating governments marked a radical rupture with Labor's tradition of democratic socialism.[16] Rather than pursuing a consensus on its own terms and setting the agenda for politics as a whole, the ALP supposedly embraced a version of elite market liberalism that elevated efficient economic management into an end in itself. Instead of Keynesian redistribution based on progressive taxation, Hawke and his treasurer, Paul Keating, stand accused of promoting a neo-liberal model of 'trickle down' wealth driven by tax cuts for the rich and a strong dose of deregulation and privatisation. And instead of collective agency rooted in the labour movement, the Hawke-Keating government is accused of individualist rather than socialist principles, neglecting solidarity, and inaugurating a new settlement that was eagerly embraced by the Liberals under Howard. As Graham Maddox and Tim Battin assert: "The Hawke Government is aware of its constituency, and once did a great job in creating work, controlling inflation and providing family welfare. It is the broader vision of a cooperative, harmonious society – the democratic-socialist vision – that has been set aside".[17] This is a caricature of what really happened.

The Maddox and Battin narrative fails on at least two counts. One is that it was Whitlam who took democratic socialism in a social-democratic direction by advocating a more liberal and secular agenda of social liberalism, which contrasted with the social conservatism of broad sections of the Australian working class. His party reforms were much-needed but they widened the gulf between the ALP's blue-collar core and its growing middle-class electorate, which would come back to haunt Labor. Whitlam's credentials as a social democrat rather than a democratic socialist were underlined by his approach to economic policy. He once said that that nationalisation was "the Old Testament" whereas he preferred "the New Testament". His decision to cut tariffs antagonised large sections of the trade union movement.

Of course, Whitlam's record in office stands in the proud tradition of radically reforming Labor governments: a national health scheme, urban and regional development, environmental protection, consumer rights, more accessible university education, a boost to needs-based financial support for schools, more Aboriginal rights, greater gender equality, and expanded childcare benefits – all underpinned by a deeply egalitarian social progressivism that entrenched the radically moderate mediating tradition. There is little doubt that Whitlam transformed the party structures and was a towering figure in the wider labour movement. On his death in 2014, Barry Jones – a former MP and President of the federal ALP – declared that Whitlam's fearless leadership "reminded us that there was a time, and there was a Leader who could transform Australian society – shatter old beliefs, look towards transcendent possibility and tell a story to be proud of".[18] In this sense, for all his technocratic modernisation, Whitlam also encapsulated the Labor tradition of ethical socialism.

The other count on which the narrative about Hawke and Keating's apparent betrayal of democratic socialism breaks down is the ethical outlook underpinning the governments they led, which was to modernise a sclerotic economy while preserving and even strengthening its social base. Nowhere is this more visible than in the Accord between the trade unions and the government. Its significance can hardly be overstated: as a former trade union leader, Hawke was uniquely positioned to persuade the unions to accept a social wage, which involved trading some wage restraint in exchange for benefits provided by the federal government. The Accord achieved a balance between national and sectional interests, and it was a concrete expression of Hawke's own moral commitment inspired by his father, Arthur Clemence 'Clem' Hawke, who had been both General Secretary of the ALP in the South Australia, 1919-20, and a Congregational church minister. Upon his father's death, Bob Hawke remarked that "he's passed on to me the fundamental beliefs I have, and that is: we are in this world not just to advance our own interests but we owe an obligation to our fellow human beings".[19] This ethical outlook shaped Hawke's twin promise "to be the leader for the whole nation" and to help build an economic democracy through parliament in line with Labor's historic mission: "What stands out is the Labor Party's capacity for change and renewal in a world of immense change, throughout a century of unprecedented change; and yet, at the same time, the consistency with which it has held to the fundamental principle: the pursuit of its program through parliamentary democracy".[20]

Crucially, the Accord built on Australia's model of industrial relations, unique in the Western world: it has deep roots in the social justice tradition of the Christian churches, as this chapter shows in relation to the 1907 *Harvester Case* on the minimum wage. That case was shaped by the first social encyclical, *Rerum Novarum* of 1891, and its emphasis on the living wage, which Hawke himself described as "the ground-breaking philosophy of *Rerum Novarum*",[21] as will be explained below in some detail. All this suggests that Labor's understanding of socialism is ethical and as such fundamentally different from the materialism of revolutionary socialist thinking prevalent among both state socialists and totalitarian communists.

Liberal and conservative elements in the ALP's philosophy

If one constitutive component of Labor's social democracy is ethical socialism, liberal political ideas are another key influence on the ALP's governing philosophy. At first this seems counter-intuitive, as the liberal emphasis on the primacy of the individual appears to be irreconcilable with the priority of the collective in Labor's ideals. Far from being a merely theoretical point, this plays into long-standing debates in Australia between free trade and protection, as well as the broader balance of individual freedoms versus the extension of state power. In each case, Labor had a complicated relationship with liberalism. In Victoria, Labor was strongly protectionist. In NSW a more open, fair trade perspective was promoted. The influence of the radical liberal and MP Bernhard Ringrose Wise KC was significant in shaping the perspective of Labor's first few decades in NSW.[22] One might further observe that the kind of progressivism promoted by the ALP had a number of illiberal or even anti-liberal traits, including opposition to liberal individualism and to a laissez-faire economy of private big business and free trade, which were seen as reactionary positions. A progressive politics required state regulation and even certain forms of paternalism in order to bring about a more just social order. This actually was part of an Australian consensus, a conception of society on which many members of the elites and the people agreed in the period from the end of World War I until the 1960s.

Historically, as Greg Melleuish has shown, the political battles in Australia did not primarily pit liberals against conservatives but rather liberals against protectionists, and even populists who were variously right-wing or left-wing.[23] As manufacturing industries grew in Australia, including in NSW, so too did a protectionist sentiment. In this sense, Labor's support for protectionism and statist paternalism put it squarely in opposition to political liberalism. As a result, the ALP's governing philosophy was not aligned with the struggle to establish liberal institutions, promote free trade, and provide a constructive alternative to populist policies such as protectionist tariffs, imperial preference, or the White Australia Policy, all of which were defended for many decades by the ALP until Whitlam changed the party's position. One reason why totalitarian state socialism neither succeeded in Australian politics nor took over the Labor Party is the bulwark provided by the country's and the party's liberal constitution.

It does not follow that Labor's political or policy platform was somehow anti-liberal until the 1960s. Rather, the influence of liberal ideas on the ALP took the form of social egalitarianism. Labor was in the business of picking and choosing. As one federal MP, Andrew Leigh, recently remarked:

> social liberalism already underpins many of Labor's achievements. Broad-based income taxation under Curtin. The Racial Discrimination Act under Whitlam. Trade liberalisation and a floating dollar under Hawke. Enterprise bargaining and native title under Keating. Removal of much of the explicit discrimination against same-sex couples under Rudd. Emissions trading and disability reform under Gillard. At last month's election, our platform included an Australian republic, a national integrity commission, tax reform, competition reform and a Future Asia plan to engage with the region. Whether through support for individual liberties or the belief of open markets, social liberalism has a prominent place in the story of the Australian Labor Party.[24]

This is but the secular progressive side of the ALP that leaves out other sources of Labor ideas on equality and freedom. As already mentioned, one influential source were the Chartists from England and Wales who brought notions of radical democracy to Australia, for example the Chartist leaders John Frost, Zephaniah Williams, and William Jones, who were taken to Tasmania after the Newport Rising of 1839. In the 1850s, Chartist demands for male suffrage and secret ballots were adopted in Victoria in the aftermath of the Eureka Stockade. Chartism as a creed straddled the divide between religious and secular thinking: Christian Chartists were critical of the Church of England's association with the establishment and they believed Christianity was above all a practice that should infuse every walk of life.

Another source of social egalitarianism was the classical liberal tradition of John Locke and Adam Smith, whose works were readily available and extensively read in Australia.[25] Their ideas were in far greater demand than those of Jeremy Bentham. To the extent that utilitarianism shaped Australian public debate, it was William Paley's more conservative strand rather than Bentham's more radical brand, as Chris Berg has shown. These findings qualify the influential thesis by Hugh Collins that Australia was predominantly a 'Benthamite society' and that utilitarianism was the prevalent public philosophy.[26] In reality, as Greg Melleuish and Stephen Chavura suggest, Australia utilitarianism was profoundly religious. For this reason it tempered the more secular positivist outlook of both Bentham and Mill's philosophy.[27] Of course, it is true that on the whole the labour movement was more shaped by radical ideas than Paley's support for the established order and his opposition to political and economic reform. But his defence of gradual and institutionally mediated change resonated with the ALP, as did his focus on self-governing individuals. To quote Berg: "Paley's emphasis on individual autonomy and moral choice is starkly different from Bentham's rationalistic paternalism. In this way, Paley bridged the philosophical radicalism of late Bentham with the philosophical conservatism of Edmund Burke, helping to develop the classical liberal political philosophy of the 19th century".[28]

The significance of this point speaks to the influence of Burkean thematics on the labour movement and the ALP: a middle path of 'radical moderation' as an alternative to timid reform or revolutionary utopia; an attention to the intergenerational bonds of solidarity between past, present, and future based on history and collective memory; a focus on society and intermediary institutions rather than the central state or the free market; the preservation of social order and representative government in the national interest; a critique of cronyism and excessive concentration of power and wealth; and, an accentuation of social virtues such as honour, loyalty, duty, and sacrifice. As Michael Easson argues, the Labor Party's governing philosophy is to bring about radical transformation in line with the country's culture and ways of life.[29] That is why Labor rejects merely marginal reform or whole revolutionary overthrow in favour of structural, systemic change – as with Bede Nairn's account of 'civilising capitalism' as Labor's historic mission.[30]

For Easson, the ALP's commitment to transform the capitalist system within the framework of parliamentary democracy, based on notions of social order, explains the party's enduring concern with "here and now needs of the workers, their families and supporters" – rather than a bourgeois defence of vested interests or a spirit of utopian revolution.[31] Such a realist focus on the present is not at the expense of the past or the future. On the contrary, the union movement and the ALP have always had a strong sense of history and their particular mission to change the social conditions of the labour interest. Connected with this is a self-understanding of Labor as a tradition, which provides continuity and holds together different habits of thought and practice. A sense of tradition is crucial because, as Stuart MacIntyre writes: "it fuses deed and memory, imaginative possibility and action, to proclaim tradition as a guide to action".[32]

In fact, there is an implicit Burkean dimension in Labor's conception of tradition, notably Burke's idea of a partnership between the dead, the living, and those to be born. Graham Maddox puts this well: Labor's tradition "looks backward and forward at the same time. . . . In so far as it dwells in the past, it understands the nature of what has gone before to constitute what exists at present".[33] Far from being monolithic, Labor's tradition is plural and encompasses elements drawn from socialism, liberalism, and conservatism, just as the ALP's history involves both continuity and discontinuity. Linking these disparate strands is the party's belief in lived fraternity as a "principled practice" that gives content to both liberty and equality. What binds workers and the communities together is what makes people free and society more just.

One of the sources of Labor's commitment to pluralism and tolerance is Burke's legacy in Australia.[34] Some of his thinking laid the foundation for reconciling sectarian divisions, something Labor has aspired for, even if it has often fallen short. The background to this noble ambition is the influence of Burkean ideas on the philosophical outlook of some of its main public figures, for example Captain Arthur Phillip, founding Governor of New South Wales, the first colony in Australia, who embraced Burke's Whig spirit of reform and humanism and was committed to bringing together estranged interests. Another example is

William Charles Wentworth who shared Burke's belief in the principle of a 'mixed constitution'.

Moreover, Burke's relative, Richard Bourke, was Governor of New South Wales from 1831 to 1837. Before coming to Australia, he had spent his holidays at Burke's home and assimilated his Old Whig philosophy (and in retirement helped to edit his uncle's correspondence). During his time in New South Wales, Bourke applied Old Whig principles in his efforts to transform the penal colony into a more self-governing polity, which included bringing back trial by jury, advocating a free press, publishing public accounts, and defending the rights of prisoners. Bourke's major achievement was the Church Act of 1836, which gave official recognition not only to Anglicanism but also to the Catholic, Presbyterian, and Wesleyan Methodist churches – many years before the Catholic hierarchy was acknowledged in England.[35]

Burke emerges as a key inspiration for some aspects of the ALP's governing philosophy on account of his fusion of traditional ideas with radical thinking – reflecting his identity as an Old Whig who was both a conservative and a liberal. A hybrid of Protestant, Irish, and Quaker ideals animated his campaign for the tolerance of Catholics in Ireland and Britain; his fight for self-government in America, and the need for conciliation with the newly independent United States; his passionate defence of the rights of Indians against colonial oppression and exploitation; and his implacable opposition to the tyranny of the French Revolution. Binding together Burke's philosophy is his profound sympathy for the victims of arbitrary power precisely because he believed that universal standards of justice and humanity are mediated through particular practices and institutions. These ideas and sentiments resonate with the moderate left, including Australian Labor.

As Isaac Kramnick has shown, the socialist thinker Harold Laski praised Burke "as one of Britain's earliest and most articulate foes of colonialism. His instinctive defence of tradition enabled Burke to see the inherent injustice of Western imperialism. The Socialist Left applauds the traditionalist Right as they both condemn the barbarism and brutality of the bourgeois age".[36] However harsh the language about the bourgeoisie, there is no doubt the ALP shares with Burke a sentiment of deep revulsion against the injustice of capitalist empire. His defence of human liberty and social advancement also resonates deeply with Labor's progressive outlook.

While being perhaps the most prescient critic of the Revolution and the unfolding tyranny in France, Burke equally opposed corporate power and an overweening state in England. His political philosophy is an alternative to liberal individualism with roots in Locke and also to the slide into collectivism whose origins can be traced to Hobbes and Rousseau.[37] Burke rejects abstract universal principles as absolutist and lacking in historical and cultural mediation. In reality, both values and institutions are anchored in moral sentiments of sympathy, generosity, and affection. Human beings are embodied beings, not rational utility maximisers, and they are embedded in relationships and institutions bound by habit, identity, and interest. Burke's emphasis on the social nature of human beings means that affection for others endows relationships with meaning. It forges attachments and helps to build both trust and cooperation. Founded upon a philosophy in which the particular serves the universal, a Burkean-inspired politics can balance principle with practice – a commitment to the virtue of justice combined with compromise and common sense. Prudence is perhaps the most cardinal of all 'principled practices', and it has certainly characterised many Labor leaders and framed their action: Curtin's careful combination of patriotism with internationalism; Hawke's fight for Indigenous recognition and progressive patriotism; and Keating's commitment to greater individual freedoms as well as mutual obligations.

Tracing in detail the various ways in which Burkean ideas have shaped Labor's governing philosophy exceeds the scope of this book. But based on the general point that Burke's considerable influence on Australian politics took the form of advocating a trustee model of political representation rather than a model of mere delegation, it is the case that the ALP has been staunch in its defence of representative government and the sovereignty of parliament based on the idea of a social order. The primary duty of MPs is to hold in balance the representation of their constituents and of the national interest, not just their voters, and to think for themselves and exercise judgement rather than slavishly follow opinions or fashions. Labor in Australia could loosen its habits and require a variant of the three-line whip rule as applies in the UK parliament without requiring every parliamentary vote (outside of the conscience vote) to be decided by caucus. This would return to a position espoused in Labor's earliest years in the Australian parliament.[38] Burke's philosophy is one of the inspirations for Labor's attempt to represent the national character and not to be beholden to sectional interest.

Nor is the influence of Burkean ideas an anachronistic projection onto the past. On the contrary, a series of senior Labor figures have referenced Burke – for example Arthur Calwell on the functioning of democratic representation, the rule of law, and the role of parties in politics.[39] Calwell also contested the idea that the Liberal Party was the main or even sole bastion of small-c conservative values in Australia. He was critical of some of the post-war developments connected with the 'permissive society', saying that it "panders to the selfish, the licentious and the avaricious; it glorifies crime, exploits sex and encourages violence".[40] By contrast, for Calwell, part of Labor's identity is its defence of large families and some socially conservative values. Barry Jones, a former Labor MP and former ALP President, has certainly promoted a more socially progressive outlook than Calwell; but he too invoked Burke – indirectly in his maiden speech in the Victorian Parliament in 1972, when he emphasised fraternity, sense of community, common human interest, human frailty, and interdependence:

> The Liberal Party in itself is a paternalistic party which has relied so much on the leadership image, whereas the Labor Party in this sense has always tried to be fraternal. . . .
>
> I am . . . a Christian Socialist influenced by Methodism rather than Marxism . . . out of my Christian concern I have, I hope, developed some kind of sense of community and a sense of common human interest which rises above party interests, even in this place.
>
> [The point is] to recognize the frailty of the human situation and that we are all weak. We all have grave weaknesses and we are inter-dependent on each other.[41]

Similarly, in a speech to the Commonwealth Parliament in 1979, Jones accentuated the importance of representative democracy and the duties of MPs, including the importance of upholding deep moral convictions that reflect a certain national character. He said this:

> Just as I respect the right of others to their conscientious position, I expect others to grant me the same right. I have agonised over the question for many years. I intend to vote against the Lusher motion and, in addressing my own electors, I adopt the words of Edmund Burke: "Your representative owes you, not his industry only, but his judgment: and he betrays instead of serving you if he sacrifices it to your opinion".[42]

Many years later, Jones commented that the Burkean emphasis on the social embeddedness of human beings and the civic covenant between generations is important for progressive politics: "The traditional/conservative view (set out with prophetic insight by Edmund Burke in October 1790) was to see man/woman in a received social context . . . People are born with a history, the product of organic processes . . .".[43] Burke's famous dictum that "a state without the means of some change is without the means of its conservation" underpins Labor's paradox of radically moderate reform that is perhaps best expressed by the notion of 'civilising capitalism'.

Two particular reforms by the ALP that embody elements of Burke are, first of all, the introduction of a universal health insurance system (first called Medibank and then Medicare), which was originally championed by the Minister for Social Security, Bill Hayden, in the government of Gough Whitlam, and then restored by the Hawke government.[44] Secondly, the creation of a national system of compulsory superannuation during the Hawke-Keating era, which strongly qualified their economic liberalism. As Mary Easson has documented, Burke's name can be cited in making the case for superannuation, in particular the Burkean idea of a civic covenant between the living, the dead, and those yet to be born,[45] or, to use more progressive language, intergenerational solidarity and justice.

In addition to Calwell and Jones, Michael Easson is one of the most prominent advocates of the Burkean conservative-liberal tradition within the ALP:

> If I were to sum up what I believe in, I would find it very hard to put it in terms which would label me a left-winger or a right-winger. In different respects I am a social democrat, a liberal, a conservative, in the various issues I confront. I think that I'm part of the tradition of the labour movement and its principles. To me our historic role, whether as part of the Left of the labour movement, however that might be defined, or as part of the movement's Centre or Right, is to civilise capitalism. I think that is an important task; it's sometimes been an heroic task for many of our forebears. It's a never-ending task, and one which I think we have a duty to share.[46]

In an essay written in May 2019, Easson argues that there are four Burkean principles that resonate deeply with the ALP's governing philosophy:

1. Appreciation for the tension between liberty and tradition, including existing institutions and values;

2. Amelioration, rather than expropriation or extirpation as the default reform approach;

3. An inclination to support more significant change so long as the horses do not run off with the cart, the cart breaks apart, or the system;

4. Keenness to extend the sphere of liberty and independence of action.

All these principles are compatible with and, indeed, have always been integral to the social democratic project.[47]

In summary, the ALP's philosophical outlook is Burkean insofar as the party tries to hold in balance modernity and tradition, individual rights and mutual obligations, and advancement and existing institutions, as well as liberty and sympathy for the victims of arbitrary power. Some of these values and sentiments may be more conservative than liberal, and the small-c conservative tradition that is a part of the Australian labour movement has been in retreat for some time; but there is no doubt that it shaped Labor's philosophy for much of the party's history. The same applies to Catholic social teaching, distributism, and cognate strands in the social justice tradition of the Christian churches, as the following section suggests.

Labor ethos

The social justice tradition of the churches, which shaped the ALP's ethical outlook, has both Protestant and Catholic roots. For decades, Christian ideas framed the fight for economic justice, social reform, and Australia's political autonomy. As Wayne Hudson has shown,

> Primitive Methodists and Bible Christians were leading advocates of social reform towards the end of the nineteenth century, providing many of the founding members of the first Parliamentary Labor Party, while nonconformists contributed to the establishment of civil liberties in South Australia. Presbyterians and Congregationalists also accepted a Christian duty to improve society and took part in education and political life.[48]

Just as not all religion in Australia was political, so too all politics in Australia was not religious. Both the country's society and polity, however, had Christian foundations well into the 1960s. The main components of Australia's values and identity are shaped by Christian values and identity – including love of the land and family, an attachment to work, affection for mates, scepticism about authority, and opposition to privilege.[49] A certain irreverent national temper was less a wholesale rejection of Christian beliefs than it was a deep scepticism about many aspects of organised religion and the clerical establishment. The enduring influence of sectarianism on politics reinforced anti-clerical sentiments, but the sheer diversity of Australian Protestantism means that the range and depth of Christian contributions to national life is as hard to appreciate as it is difficult to deny – notably ideas of social justice that animated the creation of schools, hospitals, and other civic institutions.

The endurance of Christian dispositions is also reflected in the writings of the socialist Henry Lawson mentioned earlier in this chapter. He formulated the Australian creed in terms that transcend the binary between the religious and the secular by equating Christianity with humanism and elevating the labour movement into a new universal faith:

> Trade unionism is a new and grand religion; it recognizes no creed, sect, language or nationality; it is a universal religion – it spreads from the centres of European civilization to the youngest settlements on the most remote portions of the earth; it is open to all and will include all – the Atheist, the Christian, the Agnostic, the Unitarian, the Socialist, the Conservative, the Royalist, the Republican, the black, and the white, and a time will come when all the 'ists', 'isms', etc., will be merged and lost in one great 'ism' – the unionism of labour.[50]

This philosophy was espoused and developed by William Guthrie Spence, also mentioned earlier. There was thus a convergence between socialist and Christian thinking that influenced the labour movement – transmitted through the writings of the Christian Socialists such as F. D. Maurice, Charles Kingsley, and William Temple who were all widely read and referenced by influential Australian figures such as the Anglo-Catholic Father Gerard Kennedy, the Bishop of Armidale John Moyes, and Bishop Ernest Henry Burgmann.[51] Compared with secular state socialism, Christian socialism is ethical and shifts the emphasis away from bureaucratic statism to the self-governing intermediary institutions of civil society. This is instrumental to Labor's philosophy of radical moderation and its commitment to the market economy and parliamentary democracy.

Some aspects of Christian socialism can also be found in Catholic social teaching and distributism, which over time became a major source of the ALP's philosophical outlook. The main moral principle of Catholic social teaching is the dignity of the person, which in turn is the foundation of the other principles of the common good, subsidiarity, participation, and solidarity. The dignity of the person can be defined as the intrinsic worth of each and every human being with his or her inalienable rights and duties, which implies that humans are neither administrative units nor tradable commodities but free and responsible beings. The common good is an ordering of relationships in a way that holds in balance individual fulfilment with mutual flourishing based on the dignity and equality of all people. This involves both a materially secured and meaningful life. Subsidiarity concerns the balance between personal freedom and social assistance at the most appropriate level – person, family, intermediary institution, market, state, international organisation – in accordance with the dignity of the person and the common good. Participation in community life and in the life of the polity is about the capacity of persons and groups to partake of the institutions and processes at the heart of democracy and to make their needs and interests heard in ways that can shape democratic debate and decision-making. Solidarity encompasses the obligation on all persons and groups to advance the common good as well as the actual assistance to those in need, with a view to reducing existing inequalities of wealth, power, and status.

Taken together, these five principles have four characteristics. First of all, they have enduring value whatever the circumstances. Secondly, they are the ultimate organising logic of Catholic social teaching because they refer to social reality as a whole, including politics, the economy, law, civic institutions, and international relations. Thirdly, the four principles are indivisible and form a unity, which means that there is reciprocity, interconnection, and complementarity between them. And finally, they provide the moral reference point and guidance for Catholic social teaching in its application to particular problems.

In addition to Catholic social teaching, another body of ideas grew out of Catholicism that informed the ALP's ethical perspective – an approach known as distributism. It puts the emphasis on the distribution of ownership and power to workers. Distributism focuses on the sharing of productive assets among the people for the purpose of their greater autonomy from both centralised statism and free market fundamentalism. In line with the principle of subsidiarity, distributism promotes workplace democracy and mutual models of enterprise, which imply spreading private ownership of housing and democratic control of industry through owner-operated businesses and worker-controlled cooperatives.

In the case of the ALP, the influence of Catholic social teaching and distributism goes back to the social teachings of Cardinal Manning in England as well as Cardinal Moran and Archbishop Mannix in Australia. All three drew on Catholic social teaching and championed a series of ideas, including:

- the distribution of productive assets on as wide a social basis as possible;
- parity of status and esteem between capital and labour;
- opposition to the commodification of labour, land, and other exploitative practices;
- recognition of free association, notably workers' right to form trade unions and their right to strike;
- self-help through cooperatives and other mutualist bodies;
- rejection of state socialism in its secular, Marxist, or other extreme statist forms.

Such and similar ideas shaped the labour movement and the nascent ALP, which developed many of them into a political programme and a policy agenda.[52] At the heart of the convergence between Catholic social teaching and Labor is the principle of the dignity of work. Labour is not another commodity whose price can be left to the iron law of demand and supply in the marketplace. Workers deserve a just wage precisely because they make a contribution not only to the economy but also to society. To preserve the intrinsic value of work and enable workers to share in prosperity requires respect for the natural right to form associations with fellow workers.

Trade unions are a necessary but not a sufficient condition to ensure more dignified working conditions or just wages. It is the duty of the state to create an institutional framework in which workers and employers can negotiate on a level playing field. The final outcome is not determined by considerations of power, but also ethical concerns with the wellbeing and flourishing of workers. Both in opposition and in office, the ALP has upheld the principle of free trade unions, which animated Labor's fight against the infiltration by the Communist Party of Australia and repeated attempts to bring unions under Communist control. At the same time, the ALP defended the free association of workers against systematic attacks by the Liberal Party (and its predecessors) to curb union rights and outlaw strikes. Equally, Labor has defended the idea of a just wage that allows workers to feed themselves and their families. The living wage affords a basic level of security and comfort, which together with the public provision of housing, health, and education helps workers to participate in the good life.

It is worth remembering how fierce opposition to a national living wage has been and what a key role Catholic social teaching played in bringing about a national framework for the living wage and industrial equity – the foundations of Australia's 'fair go'. This was initially codified in the third constitutional convention of 1898 (which agreed to the conciliation and arbitration power in the Australian Constitution) and then amplified in the 1907 *Harvester Case* by Justice Henry Bournes Higgins. The judge, a radical liberal who served as Attorney General in the Labor government of John Christian Watson in 1904, was the son of a Protestant clergyman in Ulster and raised in the Wesleyan tradition. In the inaugural Bishop Manning Lecture delivered in 2010, Bob Hawke recounts those momentous events:

> In April 1891 delegates from the colonies meeting in Sydney
> for the first of three Conventions to draft a constitution for the
> proposed new nation – the Commonwealth of Australia – defeated
> a proposal to include a federal power in regard to conciliation and
> arbitration. Just a few weeks later, on 15th May 1891, Pope Leo XIII
> promulgated the papal encyclical *Rerum Novarum* (on Capital and
> Labour) which was to become a bedrock of the Church's teaching
> on social justice. Most significantly *Rerum Novarum* profoundly
> influenced the thinking of Henry Bournes Higgins, a major
> advocate for the inclusion of a federal conciliation and arbitration
> power and later the President of the Commonwealth Conciliation
> and Arbitration Court who formulated the concept of the basic
> wage in the 1907 Harvester Case.[53]

In just a few words, Hawke captures a battle for the soul of
Australia. Against liberal and conservative attempts to denigrate
the sanctity of labour, the Ulsterman Higgins forged a novel
consensus by drawing on the Catholic philosophy inspired
by papal social teaching and on Protestant philosophy, which
appealed to a coalition of Christians, new liberals, and moderate
socialists (sometimes described as guild socialists). Key to this
coalition was the capacity of Catholic and Protestant ethics to
converge around a shared ethical principle of economic justice
that could be translated into the secular practice of a just wage.[54]
Remarkably, Catholic and Christian conceptions of natural law
shaped Australia's model of industrial relations.

The coalition described above prevailed twice. Firstly in 1898,
at the third and final constitutional convention, when Higgins
narrowly secured the inclusion in the draft Commonwealth
Constitution of the power for the Commonwealth to legislate for

"conciliation and arbitration for the prevention and settlement of industrial disputes extending beyond the limit of any one State".[55] Over the next five years, it took a heroic parliamentary battle to enshrine into law a Commonwealth Court of Conciliation and Arbitration. Then, the landmark *Harvester Case* of 1907 "witnessed the ultimate fusion of the philosophy of the Pope and the philosophy and practice of the Ulsterman".[56] Hawke wanted to highlight the broad Christian foundations of such thinking – neither solely Catholic nor Protestant. As the judge of the Arbitration Court, Higgins ruled that the aim of the basic wage paid to workers is

> to secure them something which they cannot get by the ordinary system of individual bargaining with employers . . . [the standards of 'fair and reasonable' are] the normal needs of the average employee, regarded as a human being living in a civilised community . . . a condition of frugal comfort estimated by current human standards. This, then, is the primary test, the test which I shall apply in ascertaining the minimum wage that can be treated as 'fair and reasonable' in the case of unskilled labourers.[57]

Higgins's ruling applied to working families with three children and the weekly basic wage amounted to 42 shillings. This was, henceforth, the foundation for the pay structure in Australia. From 1921, the basic was automatically adjusted each quarter to reflect changes in the costs of living, but a 1953 court decision (Basic Wage Inquiry 77 CAR 477) abolished this adjustment and with it a key pillar of Catholic social teaching. The church taught that wages should enable workers to live a decent life and not simply reflect productivity gains if these are below inflation, otherwise real wages are reduced. As Hawke explains in his Manning Lecture, the work he personally did in the late 1950s and early 1960s with the Australian Council of Trade Unions managed to reverse the 1953 ruling and reinstated the link between the basic wage and the costs of living – against the express influence by one B. A. Santamaria, according to Hawke.[58]

Fast forward to the 1980s: it is now clear that the Hawke-Keating government was on the side of Catholic social teaching and associated cognate traditions in Protestantism and non-Christian ethical thinking. Indeed, the Accord and the 'social wage' reflect an ethical commitment rather than just an economic logic. In the words of Hawke himself:

> Speaking very broadly then, one can say that for the thirty year period from 1966 – when I got that principle reaffirmed – up to 1996, the fundamental principles of *Rerum Novarum*, i.e.

> A. a decent wage maintained and increased in real value to reflect both price movements and in John XXIII's words "the increased productivity", and

> B. the recognition of the rights of trade unions to work freely on behalf of their members were, broadly speaking, reflected in the Australian industrial relations system. Then came the Prime Ministership of John Howard and the emergence of Work Choices which in essence represented a regression to the pre-Federation employers rallying cry of "freedom of contract" and the rejection of an effective and legitimate role for trade unions – the very antithesis of the philosophical and spiritual foundation of *Rerum Novarum*.[59]

The implication is that the ALP's governing philosophy is true to the legacy of Christian social teaching, while the Liberal Party under Howard betrayed this spirit just when it purported to represent the interests of Catholic workers who had joined its ranks from Labor. Similarly, while serving as treasurer in the Hawke government, Paul Keating characterised the ALP's philosophical approach in this way: "Free of the shackles of any rigid ideology and remaining alive to the lessons of a changing world, there should be little that Labor cannot achieve in its quest to fulfil its original and essential charter – to improve the lot of the common people".[60]

The two fundamental issues, which Hawke and Keating's self-characterisation raises, are, first of all, how the ALP tries to combine continuity with change and, second, which traditions of political thought and practice have shaped the party's ethical outlook. This chapter suggests that Australian Labor rests on a governing philosophy of radical moderation that fuses respect for inherited institutions with a commitment to ameliorate the social conditions of workers in ways that reflect both the labour and the national interest. The ALP's philosophical approach builds on elements of democratic socialism, small-l liberalism, Burkean small-c conservatism, and the social justice tradition of the Christian churches, notably Catholic social thought and its enduring influence on the ALP via Industrial Relations as seen in the *Harvester Case*. One question that arises from this argument is this: what holds these disparate elements together and how to explain Labor's departure from its own ethical outlook?

Labor values and dispositions

Since its creation, the ALP sought to uphold a number of values, especially democracy, social justice, and the common good. Arguably, Labor values remained the same but the underlying norms have changed. If values can be described as universal, then norms are particular. Or perhaps it is better to consider values as timeless and norms as time-specific. For example, both liberty and equality are values invoked over a long period – stretching back as far as the biblical traditions and Greco-Roman philosophy. But the norms of what it means to be free and equal have changed considerably and often unrecognisably over time. The paradox about timeless values is that they are delineated by time. Universal values and the particular norms they translate into are either timely or untimely. They either reflect the prevailing zeitgeist or they do not. And they are always shape-shifting and continually shaping form.

Such changes are often unarticulated. They tend to creep up on a society largely unannounced and often un-theorised too. And a change of norms is usually very hard to accept to begin with, as with the controversial question of conscription and Curtin's evolution on this matter. Other examples in the history of the ALP include the move away from the language of socialism towards social democracy and the shift from justice to fairness. On the former, it is instructive to recall the words of William Lane, whose prose in 1894 highlighted a vision of community at the roots of Labor's radical reforming agenda: "Socialism is more a spirit and a temper than a system. It means the spirit of companionship and mateship instead of a spirit of jealous rivalry and petty personal ambition . . . The essence of true Socialism is a desire to serve others".[61] Since Whitlam, and then Hawke and Keating, references by the ALP to socialism declined in favour of social democracy, and this also marks a subtle philosophical shift from a more ideological to a more pragmatic way of doing politics. This is to focus on what works rather than on abstract ideas; but perhaps at the expense of a more clearly defined ethical position. Pluralism is now valued far more than a more rigorous conception.

On the shift from justice to fairness, a good illustration is a speech by Julia Gillard, as Deputy Prime Minister, in 2008 in which she launched a process that would culminate in the 2009 Fair Work Act under which the annual wage review is conducted. In her speech entitled, "Introducing Australia's New Workplace Relations System", Gillard said this:

> The signature values of nations are often defined by the circumstances of their birth. This is as true for Australia as for other countries. And for us there's one value above all others that we identify with as truly our own. It's the value that emerged out of the circumstances of Federation, which coincided with the industrial turbulence of the late nineteenth and early twentieth centuries. That value is fairness. Or as we like to put it: the 'fair go'. It inspired us to establish a society that aimed to give every citizen a decent standard of living. And it led us in 1907 to establish the principle of the living wage.[62]

Interestingly, in the governing philosophy of the ALP, the word justice is more prominent than fairness, which partly reflects semantic preferences but also some substantive differences that are related to natural law and justice as the pursuit of the common good, rather than the more procedural meaning of fairness, as Tim Soutphommasane has outlined.[63]

Ultimately, the ALP's philosophy will never be a Cartesian model of clarity; nor should it be. Rather, what matters for Labor's efforts to fuse principle with practice is a recognition of the party's fundamental dispositions – the moral sentiments that inform Labor's animating energy. In line with the ALP's ambition to be a party that is both national and popular and which represents the interests of labour and the nation, those sentiments are both small-c conservative and radical. These dispositions are certainly not the monopoly of political parties or ideological systems. Rather, they are qualities of mind and character that are woven into the tapestry of national culture and are an integral part of the country's social fabric. Conservatives consider traditions to be central because they transmit inherited institutions and a sense of authority, which are vital for a just social order. By contrast, liberals believe human progress frees us from oppression and exploitation and that individual will combined with reason can bring about social advancement. Australian culture is profoundly shaped by both these sentiments, which are partially complementary but also stand in tension with each other.

J. S. Mill said as much when he suggested that "every Englishman of the present day is by implication either a Benthamite or a Coleridgean".[64] Bentham was a progressive philosopher, whereas Coleridge was a conservative thinker. What Mill said about nineteenth-century England seems to apply to Australia's national culture too. Luck and legend might be a part of it, but Australian society has equally been shaped by the forging of new institutions and of a new ethos that builds on inherited traditions. The tensions and contradictions between old and new are palpable in every age, perhaps especially in a country that grew from a penal colony to a self-governing Commonwealth. As Chris Berg argues, Australia was always much more than a Benthamite society. The liberal tradition drew on Locke and Smith, while utilitarian ideas took the form of Paley's conservatism more than Bentham's radicalism.[65] To these can be added the Burkean fusion of small-l liberal with small-c conservative principles and the social justice tradition of the churches – both of which blend a commitment to radical economic justice with a more traditional conserving of family and social bonds.

Australia's paradoxical politics is embedded in its constitutional settlement and political system. The monarchy and parliamentary sovereignty constrained political extremes and mostly held the two main dispositions in balance. Similar to other Anglo-Saxon countries with their common law tradition and the historical importance of custom and mores, Australia has largely avoided mass extremist parties of both the radical right and the revolutionary left. But, in times of crisis, one sentiment has tended to dominate the other – as with the economic turmoil of the 1930s, the Communist threat in the 1950s, the need for modernisation in the 1970s and 1980s, and the global financial crash of 2007-08.

In one sense, Australia is much more stable today than at most points since 1919 and 1945. A certain crisis is unfolding, however – a crisis which is perhaps less visible but for that reason more menacing. It is a crisis of trust in political institutions and a crisis of solidarity, which has the potential to erode the foundations of Australian society. Four decades of globalisation and rapid technological change contributed to growing economic and social insecurity for many citizens. Particular problems include rising levels of loneliness, drug abuse, divorce, and single motherhood, as well as falling levels of social mobility and the worsening prospects for young people. Among certain communities, a sense of anger and abandonment is spreading. Increasing numbers of people feel humiliated, unable to live the lives they hope for, and powerless to shape the forces that dominate them and those they care about most.

Both the economy and education are sources of division rather than areas where people build a common life. Society is split between the people and those who are (and are seen as) self-serving elites. A deep distrust of (traditional forms of) authority goes hand in hand with a suspicion that those with power and wealth are remote, disconnected from the ordinary lives of most people, and incapable of providing leadership in the national interest. The rise of identity politics is fuelling even more vicious 'culture wars' than anything seen in the 1970s. Much of the West is suffering what Mark Lilla, the American liberal critic, calls a "moral panic" over sexuality, race, and gender.[66] Added to this are fears that a sense of belonging to neighbourhoods and nations is being lost. The mainstream culture celebrates the vices of greed, promiscuity, and violence, rather than the social virtues of generosity, loyalty, and cooperation.

Taken together, economic and cultural insecurity undermine the conservation of society and nature and thereby weaken the constraints holding the forces of rampant liberalism in check. The Liberal Party under John Howard began to abandon its conservative ethos in favour of liberal market fundamentalism, which is the main force eroding the socially conservative values that his party purports to uphold. Meanwhile, the ALP became increasingly socially liberal and neglected its small-c conservative disposition. The dominant elites, as the American social theorist Christopher Lasch argued nearly twenty-five years ago, are often so remote that they fail to understand or sympathise with the lives of ordinary people.[67] They lack the basic sense of belonging to people and places, and an appreciation for hard work and contribution, as well as the importance of 'reciprocal obligations' – duties towards others rather than individual entitlements. Much of national politics is an angry shouting match between libertarian free-market nationalism and cosmopolitan ultra-liberalism.

Many people are equally opposed to either option and tend to be in a middle-ground that is as economically radical as it is socially moderate. Arguably, this paradoxical disposition is expressed in a desire for a renewed ordinary culture in which human relationships, the need for belonging, and the moral practice of reciprocity are recognised. For example, much of the Australian electorate is economically radical but fiscally conservative: they want economic justice tackled and privilege abolished; but they are weary of high levels of public debt and the idea of a nation that lives beyond its means. They genuinely want the fair go for all where hard work and respect make a contribution to society that is rewarded. Most people are small-l liberals who respect cultural difference and diversity and reject discrimination or intolerance. But a majority is also socially and culturally more communitarian and even small-c conservative, valuing faith, family, community, and country. Despite the extraordinary changes over the past four decades, Australia's paradox remains unchanged. The dilemma for the ALP is whether it deftly expresses both poles of the country's paradoxical politics or not.

As this and the previous chapter suggest, Australian Labor embodies the paradox of being both radical and conservative throughout its history and in terms of its governing philosophy. In this manner lies its legitimate claim as the true national party

– precisely because it reflects the two dominant dispositions of the Australian people. Even though the ALP's time in power is a lot less than the Liberal Party in its various incarnations, Labor played a vital role in upholding the traditions of the country and shaping its modernisation. Does this still hold nowadays? The decline of the industrial working class and the rise of a new professional class of university-educated middle-class voters realigned the ALP with a predominantly urban, progressive, liberal, and cosmopolitan identity. This became increasingly influential from the late 1960s onwards, but which is less representative of the country as a whole. The danger is that Labor is – or is seen as – on the side of one section of society rather than the whole nation.

Many cosmopolitan liberals passionately believe in equality, diversity, and freedom from discrimination. This implies that mutual obligation to others should extend to all human beings, not merely fellow citizens. Justice is primarily about subjective rights and utility rather than virtue or the common good, which involve some notion of place and people rather than the whole planet. As a result, cosmopolitan liberals attach less importance to the family, the nation, and inherited cultural traditions than they ascribe to a universal creed of humanity, the globe, and a single global culture.[68] This perspective fuels 'culture wars' and identity politics, including the denigration of both Indigenous and immigrant working-class culture as well as national traditions that are accused of glorifying imperialism and racism. Here the work of Tim Soutphommasane on progressive patriotism is particularly interesting in renewing Labor's balance between its more radical and its more traditional dispositions.

If the party does not heed this, it runs the risk of privileging progress over tradition, identity over class, free choice over common endeavour, and self-expression over solidarity. Yet not all progress is good; all progress can be reversed, as the political philosopher John Gray argues.[69] What is gained can just as easily be lost, and therefore lasting advancement requires strong institutions and traditions of practice. Class has changed almost beyond recognition without disappearing altogether. It remains an important marker of people's sense of belonging. Free choice and individual emancipation are key in the continual fight against oppression and exploitation, but they do not replace collective action. And self-expression often leads to narcissism when people actually need mutual recognition of their talents, vocations, and roles in society. Lived fraternity is what makes us free and society more just.

Labor may not need any of this to win the next election. But to govern well and regain people's trust, the ALP has to avoid the path to cultural sectarianism, which would elevate its progressive disposition into an absolute while denigrating the conservative sentiment in the labour movement and the wider society. How the party can try to hold the line is the subject of the final chapter.

4

Politics and Policy
Renewing party and
country

Holding the line

After the 2019 defeat and the election of a new leader, Anthony
Albanese, the ALP will be assessed against successful attempts to
win office from opposition. This Labor managed to do only three
times since 1945: under Gough Whitlam in 1972, Bob Hawke
in 1983, and Kevin Rudd in 2007. There are several lessons from
Labor's legacy that the party needs to bear in mind. First of all, the
ALP is sometimes focused on its leader to the point of obsession.
One could call this Labor's messiah complex – the saviour who
supposedly rescues the party and the country. The other extreme was
the series of coups during the Rudd-Gillard-Rudd years, which cost
the ALP much popular trust. By contrast, Bill Shorten managed to
restore some sense of unity, which Albanese has praised – a "unity
of purpose", which shows that: "We learned the lessons of the last
time we were in government and we haven't gone back there".[1] Both

unity of purpose and collegiality will be vital, but leadership in the labour and the national interest also requires, as this chapter argues, a fundamental shift in party culture and organisation.

The second lesson is connected with the first and concerns the need to match the ALP's governing strategy to its governing philosophy. In recent times, there is the tendency towards bureaucratic administration or managerialism or some fusion of the two. But in times of economic and political polarisation, Labor's courage and imagination is needed to hold the line and offer a transformative agenda. The problem is that most policies that are glossed as radical reforms tend to involve tinkering at the margins. They are little more than evolutionary administrative processes within the existing structures. A Labor government is not radically reforming in the sense of being faithful to the party's original purpose unless the aim is to transform systems and institutions. Tax changes or new regulations are necessary but insufficient to change the prevailing paradigms and structural constraints. The dominant ideology of our time is economic and social liberalism. This provided opportunities and freedoms to many; but in its contemporary form it also leads to new levels of inequality and insecurity that feed the current backlash against the system. With trust in mainstream party politics in free fall and voter dissatisfaction on the rise, the ALP must offer a vision for the nation that translates into meaningful action. Labor must address pressing problems of properly paid work, more support for family, conserving place and community, protecting country, tackling climate change, and building international alliances. Albanese and his team know that fighting an election on a change agenda is harder than arguing for the status quo, but they understand the need for long-term, structural, real reform. The task for them is to retain a strong moral compass as they try to gain office.

This leads to the third lesson, which is about Labor's reliance on either the market or the state or some combination of the two in order to bring about fundamental change. The problem is that both state and market institutions are now too powerful and remote from ordinary people, and both are in need of profound transformation. The market has lost its ethical bearings while the state tends to be disconnected from the everyday existence of most citizens. What both require is a strong ethical outlook combined with a pluralisation, so that they can represent and reconcile the above-mentioned estranged interests. Practical, radical reforms that embody such a bold approach include worker representation on company boards, welfare reform that devolves power to local communities as well as a strong focus on vocational training and vocational labour market entry, coupled with power to trade union members and new forms of worker and civic self-organisation.

Underpinning these three legacy issues is the question of Labor's animating energy and ethical outlook. What is the party for? The key task for Albanese is to renew the ALP's original purpose and orientation towards national tradition and towards the basic aspiration of leading a good, secure and meaningful life. To do so requires primarily a courageous and confident narrative that resonates with the concerns and needs of a large majority. As Tony Judt remarked about the social-democratic left, "they need to begin by asking, how should we talk politics? Before asking, what are our policies?"[2]

On this point, Judt is right. The principal driver of popular support is not ideology or interest. It is the loyalties of social groups that are rooted in ways of life inherited across generations even when many norms evolve significantly. Social groups reflect how individuals understand their lives and the traditions and culture they inherit from their families, communities, and the country. This is expressed in Labor's Burkean, small-c conservative disposition. In their book, *Democracy for Realists*, the American political scientists Christopher Achen and Larry Bartels argue that the most important bases of political commitments and behaviour are "group ties and social identities".[3] For the great majority of citizens, politics is not primarily about assessing the policies of one party against another. It begins with the question, "Where do people like me fit in?", and then, "Which party is for people like us?" Culture is interwoven with economics because people tend to vote for redistributive policies that benefit those to whom they have a connection, which is anchored in a shared sense of belonging and solidarity.

Globalisation, the transition from an industrial to a service economy, and rapid social change linked to demography and immigration left millions of (former) Labor voters uncertain about how to answer those two questions. They do not see many politicians who share their own life experience. Nor do they trust mainstream political parties to make sense of it. ALP voters are demanding fundamental change, which corresponds to the party's radical egalitarian disposition. That is why Labor's quest to regain popular trust starts with a fundamental overhaul of party culture and organisation. In relation to this question and on the key policy issues, this chapter argues that Catholic social teaching, distributism, and cognate concepts in the social justice tradition of the other churches offer some rich resources for radical reform and policy ideas.

Party organisation

Australia's political landscape is characterised by a decline in the main party vote and the rise of the small party vote. The latter increased from just over 8 percent in 1980 to over 23 percent in 2016 and 2019. At the same time, there is growing disaffection with politics and the alienation of traditional core Labor supporters, especially those with working-class origins. Added to this is an increasingly diverse electorate and the disruption of social media, all of which makes a national conversation ever-more difficult. The professionalisation of politics and the selection of candidates from narrow socio-cultural backgrounds is not favouring the election of politicians who lead by example and make sacrifices and compromises required for solutions to the deep-seated problems facing the country. Compulsory voting and Australia's majoritarian electoral system have so far stopped any insurgent party from destabilising two-party rule altogether; but far-left or more likely radical-right populism has the potential to deny either of the two main parties a stable majority. The argument that One-Nation is little more than a temporary aberration and that politics will in time revert back to normal is not persuasive. The major party vote share is down. This is part of longer-term demographic and sociological trends. The danger is whether this leads either to a slow slide over the next decade or triggers a sudden collapse. The onus is on Labor to confront the fundamental challenge of a broken politics and economic model, and to re-imagine its original mission of giving people a share of the good life.

Catholic social teaching offers two ideas that can provide some guidance to the reform of party organisation. The first idea grows out of the duty to reconcile estranged interests and consists in the practice of reciprocity. From its inception until the 1970s, reciprocity was at the heart of the relationship between the ALP and its working-class voters, even though the history of this relationship was never linear. Each recognised itself in the other. In return for the party's commitment to honour people's work and their contribution to the country, Labor's obligation was to protect the interests of working families against the forces of dispossession. Today, the party needs to rebuild and strengthen the sense of mutual obligation. While the ALP struggles to command a two-party combined vote over 50 percent, hundreds of thousands of working-class voters have abandoned the party in favour of the Liberals and even One-Nation. Many believe that Labor broke its obligation to them and they no longer recognise the party as their own.

Connected with reciprocity is the reconciliation of the labour interest with the interest of capital in a negotiated civic settlement, starting with the party which should be pro-worker and pro-enterprise while being sceptical about big government and big business. This too is reflected in the social justice tradition of the churches and their emphasis on more relational, reciprocal, and mutualist arrangements, which put the needs and interests of persons above the impersonal forces of state administration or market management. Political parties should be embedded in the social ties and civic bonds that constitute Australian society. In realistic terms for the ALP, this means that renewal begins with listening to what people have to say and understanding what matters to them in their everyday existence, but also selecting candidates who represent their constituents and are not strangers parachuted into seats in communities they do not know.

The second idea partly derived from Catholic social teaching is community organising.[4] Its overarching principle of grassroots mobilisation is embraced by the ALP, as Tom Bentley argues.[5] Both the party's local organisation and its campaign strategy are grounded in the Community Action Network, which builds on some of Barack Obama's campaign methods modelled on community organising, notably networks of trained activists working in teams to train and coordinate new groups of volunteers who make phone calls and knock on the doors of undecided voters. In the 37 days of the 2019 election campaign, over 25,000 volunteers across the country knocked on about 800,000 doors and made around 1,000,000 phone calls. This complemented the work of party officials and members, as well as digitally based campaigns by candidates themselves. Together with affiliated trade unions and their members, community organisations have the capacity to tap into a network of citizens to create a powerful campaigning operation without which Labor cannot win.[6]

Compared with the age of Clinton and Blair, Australian Labor renewed its campaign strategy by avoiding constant changes to the brand and new messages based on narrow focus groups. Such methods tend to leave voters confused and reinforce a deep distrust of the party's commitment to its fundamental values.[7] Instead, the ALP tried to focus on restoring Australia's fair go – the promise of economic justice and social solidarity that was betrayed by the Liberal Party in power. But Labor did not develop a narrative that could balance a working-class concern for insecure jobs with attention to middle-class aspiration. Moreover, as Bentley rightly remarks, the party's strategy "has not dealt with Australian Labor's great vulnerability: its inability to move beyond factionalised machine-based decision-making in its own forums and structures, including national and state conferences, selection of candidates for public office, and overall party administration".[8] Political parties represent communities or coalitions of interests. The danger is that Labor becomes a machine that just talks to itself.

Of course, factions are a party-political reality and they continue to play a key role in transmitting different intellectual traditions and dispositions – the moral sentiments that make up Labor's character. Indeed the factional structure is a genuinely distinctive feature of the ALP. It allows, for example, the Shop Distributive and Allied Employees' Association (SDA) group to have its own socialisation process distinct from the socially liberal mainstream of the party for a portion of trade unionists and young Labor people. More generally, the factions also help to organise caucus and the operation of the ALP at both federal and state levels. The Right faction tempered ideological and personal conflict, which was vital in ensuring the longevity of the Labor government led by Hawke and then Keating. Paradoxically, the factional system of Left and Right ossified just as old ideological positions began to dissolve in the post-Cold War era. In relation to communism, both factions lost their raison d'être. The Left struggled to make the case for democratic socialism, while the Right was increasingly divided between more liberal and conservative views, especially but not exclusively among Catholics and other Christians. "In place of an ideologically coherent Right and the Centre-Left's demise", Nick Dyrenfurth argues, "a balkanised factional system has emerged based less around ideas and more around shifting alliances between unions and leading personalities, often formed in the toxic world of student politics".[9]

Yet one might also observe that the factional structure of the ALP is aided by the revulsion against the far left that many young Labor right people, beyond the SDA, acquire through student politics. Without a factional home they might leave the ALP altogether. This is an aspect of the dynamic that Dyrenfurth does not capture in his reference to what can be the toxified environment at some university campuses. Even so, the factional system of Left and Right is all too frequently part and parcel of an organisational culture that is top-down, closed, often dominated by vested interests, and lacking in broader engagement, more civic participation, and a periodic renewal of ideas and party structures. This is another aspect of the progressive dilemma of modern politics. One fear is that if the ALP became a mass party like UK Labour, the far Left would take over. Burkean ideas about MPs owing a duty to their electorates to think for themselves would be diminished. Even the conscience vote could be in jeopardy, as the next section discusses.

In 2014, Shorten sought to transform the party into a membership-based movement with popular participation through a series of measures, including a one-click online membership category, a stronger say for members in pre-selection, the promise of greater rank-and-file contribution to National Conference, which is Labor's main policy-making forum, and an extension to state and territory branches of the 50:50 system (caucus and members) used to elect the federal leader. These changes failed to boost membership from the current level around 50,000 to the target of 100,000. In short, in a country of over 27 million, Labor is no mass movement. Bentley is right to warn that without significant change, "the wider bonds between political organisation, civil society, workplaces and citizen participation are being lost".[10] Therefore, Labor in opposition needs to revisit party reform as a matter of priority, especially by selecting candidates representing both older and newer ALP voters, so that it can once more win power.

Party culture

Beyond organisational change, Labor needs cultural change too. In his influential book, *The Righteous Mind*, the political psychologist Jonathan Haidt identifies six moral intuitions that can be found in virtually all cultures. They are care, fairness, liberty, loyalty, authority, and sanctity. The ALP has an increasingly liberal-progressive culture that emphasises care and fairness which are important principles. But even its notion of fairness is distributive justice based on need, in contrast to the view shared by many – perhaps a majority in Australia – that justice is reciprocal and based on contribution. Labor values liberty but more and more in the sense of free choice and absence of constraints on individual volition, rather than the freedom to pursue moral ends and render obligations to others. The ALP respects authority in terms of party leadership and some national institutions, but less so in relation to society and culture. Much of the party does not attach great importance to loyalty and even less so to sanctity.

This marks a break with the ethical traditions in the Labor Party and the wider labour movement. During the debate on the *Voluntary Assisted Dying Bill 2017* in Victoria, Paul Keating made this point, and it is worth quoting him at some length:

> No matter what justifications are offered for the bill, it constitutes an unacceptable departure in our approach to human existence and the irrevocable sanctity that should govern our understanding of what it means to be human . . . What matters is the core intention of the law. What matters is the ethical threshold being crossed. What matters is that under Victorian law there will be people whose lives we honour and those we believe are better off dead . . .
>
> An alarming aspect of the debate is the claim that safeguards can be

provided at every step to protect the vulnerable. This claim exposes the bald utopianism of the project – the advocates support a bill to authorise termination of life in the name of compassion, while at the same time claiming they can guarantee protection of the vulnerable, the depressed and the poor. No law and no process can achieve that objective . . .

Opposition to this bill is not about religion. It is about the civilisational ethic that should be at the heart of our secular society. The concerns I express are shared by people of any religion or no religion. In public life it is the principles that matter. They define the norms and values of a society and in this case the principles concern our view of human life itself. It is a mistake for legislators to act on the deeply held emotional concerns of many when that involves crossing a threshold that will affect the entire society in perpetuity.[11]

In addition to sanctity broadly defined, Labor also struggles to respect religious belief. People of faith increasingly question whether the ALP respects their views, particularly where they clash with the prevailing social liberalism. Not that people of faith are excluded from Labor's ranks. Brian Howe, Deputy Prime Minister, 1991-95 under Hawke and Keating, was a former Methodist Minister. Former Senator Michael Tate, Minister for Justice, 1987 to 1993 under Hawke and Keating, was President of the Parliamentary Christian Fellowship, 1985 to 1988. After retirement from politics he studied for the priesthood and was ordained in 2012. He is now a priest of the parish of the Huon Valley in Tasmania and Diocesan Consultor to the Archbishop of Hobart. But there seem to be fewer people of such backgrounds drawn to, becoming active in, and eventually seeking to represent Labor.

Given the times, a party like Labor is likely to be mostly socially liberal, but within its support base are people holding to a myriad of deeply held, sometimes religiously inspired beliefs on matters of conscience. For example, on late-term abortion, abortion more generally, same-sex marriage, surrogacy, and new areas of biotechnology such as stem-cell research. Opinions on each of those questions sometimes vary, even between people who consider themselves faithful to their church. The conscience vote within the ALP was under threat, as was foreshadowed at the 2016 national ALP conference and by some elements of the party in state and territory branches. The new ALP leader, Anthony Albanese, however, soon after he was elected in 2019 defended the right of ordinary party members, and MPs, to vote according to conscience.

People of faith, ALP members and supporters, need to know that in the Labor coalition there is a place for them. Labor needs to reach out to all people of faith. Adherents are usually concerned to assist their communities, seek improvement in the lives of their members, those they know and the strangers in their midst. They provide a helping hand to those ill, alone, and suffering from disability. Their idealism is something Labor can tap into. Indeed, Labor needs every soul it can get.

For the ALP to win a majority, it must be a home for believers, too. They are not limited to the traditional working-class base that is often religious and more socially conservative, but extends to ethnic minorities – especially recent migrants. Andrew West writes:

> Labor, and the broader left, need to understand that you cannot celebrate multiculturalism without supporting religious freedom. Internal ALP research shows that the best indicator of a person's willingness to vote Labor is how recently they migrated to Australia. The census tells us that the best indicator of how religiously observant a person is, is how recently they migrated to Australia.[12]

West makes the important point that Labor should be the natural party for religious people because the party champions individual rights and the dignity of the person, which includes religious freedom. Yet the ALP is ambiguous about protecting the freedom to believe and practice one's faith in private and public, while at the same time professing to defend Australia's pluralist democracy. Labor's lack of commitment to religious freedom alienates a significant part of the population – "people whose faith affirms their work and whose work affirms their faith". According to the National Church Life Survey, the biggest survey outside of the census, 41 percent of people who worship regularly vote for the Coalition, compared with only 26 percent for the ALP. West is right to ask: "How many would be . . . open to voting for the ALP and its egalitarian economic agenda if not for fears about religious freedom?".[13]

Freedom of religion, free conscience, and a concern for our human nature also resonate deeply with the spiritual beliefs of Aboriginal and Torres Strait Islander people. In a remarkable speech on assisted suicide in 2018, the ALP Senator Patrick Dodson explains how

> In Yawuru we have three concepts that guide our experience of life. They shape our ways of knowing and understanding, and are the collective approach to our existence on this earth and, to that extent, any afterlife that may come. They are: mabu ngarrungu(nil), a strong community – the wellbeing of all is paramount; mabuburu, a strong place and a good country – human behaviour and needs must be balanced in their demands and needs of what creation provides; and mabu liyan, a healthy spirit and good feeling. Individual wellbeing and that of our society not only have to be balanced but be at peace with each other within the context of our existence and experience.[14]

Dodson goes on to argue that these three principles rest on a relational conception of life that involves mutual obligations towards others and the whole of society. This means valuing the relationships which embed us and make us human – caring for loved ones and honouring fellow human beings:

> This concept of interconnectedness is one that transcends across many First Nations groups. It is grounded in our understanding that human resilience is based on our relationships with each other and our connectedness with the world around us. The quality of life for individuals and for our communities are intertwined, not limited to the wellbeing of an individual. We are fundamentally responsible for honouring our fellow human beings. We are called to carry responsibilities, to exercise duties and to honour those who are in need, who are ill, who are elderly, who are dependent and those of the next generation to value life with love, respect and responsibility. This is true of family members and unknown individuals. Moving away from such principles and values begins to reshape the value of human beings and our civil society, in my view.[15]

Crucially, Dodson emphasises our common humanity as a shared transcendent horizon. Life transcends private self-possession and individual volition. Individual rights cannot override the mutual obligations we owe to one another:

> We exist not as solitary individuals; we exist within a family, a community, our cultures and ethos, and in the kinship landscape. I'm a great admirer of those who have cared for loved ones and made personal sacrifices to do so. Not everyone is able to do this, I know, and I do not condemn them for the choices that they make. In the broad sense, we are part of a common humanity. If we give one person the right to make that decision – that is, to assist in committing suicide – we as a whole are affected. If we give one family that right, we as a whole are affected. If we give one state or territory that right, we as a country are affected. If we give one nation

the right to determine life, our common humanity is affected. I cannot support this legislation.[16]

What does this mean for Labor? To regain the trust of ordinary people and enlist more of them as members, the party has to balance the radical outlook of liberal progressivism with the more communitarian outlook of small-c conservatism – less Mill and more Burke. The former is important in the fight against the Liberal Party's libertarian drift, but it is insufficient in order to represent the values governing people's everyday experience – love and care for family and friends, attachment to place, as well as loyalty to community and country. These values are key to creating political agency and giving power to the powerless. For a Labor politics to grow out of the experiences of ordinary life, it has to open itself up to the full range of moral intuitions. What are the different social groups that constitute the labour interest? How can the party renew its politics around a balance of interests? It will not find the answers in abstract ideals, nor in the bureaucratic managerialism of social democratic tax-and-spend politics, nor in the rationalistic individual market choice of liberalism.

As Chapter 3 suggested, Labor needs a revitalised public political philosophy to build a broad coalition of social groups that can share a sense of national community. In addition to implementing its main policy pledges, it also needs to make an understanding of identity and belonging and of how groups work, more central to how it conducts a national conversation. Individuals are social beings made in the culture of the social groups they belong in, as Burke insisted. Then, as now, they make their political allegiances to affirm their identity. To win them over, the ALP has to recognise its diverse social groups and their respective cultural values and begin a dialogue even when it involves incompatible points of view on certain issues. We are back to the balance between the two traditions and dispositions, which are synthesised in the party's paradoxical idea of radical moderation and the conception of justice as the virtuous practice of give-and-take – contribution and reward, rather than simply individual entitlement and top-down distribution.

The democratic practice of the common good, Labor's original purpose, is about forging a shared commitment to the institutions that reflect Australia's national common life. It is about building relationships, working with estranged interests, and engaging with cultural, religious, and ethnic tensions so as to improve social integration. It calls for a revival of democratic politics with its power struggles, deals, and compromises. To renew itself, Labor must exchange its transactional politics for fostering social ties and doing things with people, not to them or for them. Its politics and policies need to be shaped by values widely shared by Australians: family, hard work, fairness, contribution, and patriotism. These values do not need qualifications such as 'progressive' or 'conservative'. They are beyond binaries and reflect the national character. With the party's priority being jobs and growth, the starting point is economic justice.

Economic justice: raising wages and spreading ownership

Superficially, Australia's economy should be a source of pride for Australians and the envy of the world: 28 years of uninterrupted growth, historically low interest rates, and levels of unemployment at 5 percent or less. But beneath the surface the reality for most people is very different. Amid increasing inequalities of wealth, power, and status, many Australians sense that the dominant economic model does not work for them. The paradoxes are stark: a richer country but greater economic insecurity; low unemployment but increasingly precarious jobs; high employment but low pay. As the increase in the costs of living regularly outstrips wage growth, real income stagnation and even decline is undoubtedly the single most pressing problem facing working Australians, combined with the fear of losing or not getting a secure job. Labor has rightly made sluggish economic growth, job insecurity, and stagnant wages, especially for people on the lowest incomes, the central plank of its political platform and policy agenda.

What is particularly significant is that the ALP seems to draw on an idea derived from Catholic social teaching – the living wage.[17] A *living wage* is an economic and an ethical concept, whereas the *minimum wage* is determined by law or by a public agency such as the Fair Work Commission. The reason why Labor committed to the living wage is because the national minimum wage is little more than a safety net that has not prevented people in full-time work from experiencing poverty. *In-work poverty* is the technocratic phrase for a life devoid of dignity. Rather than just topping up insufficient wages with tax credits or other instruments, the ALP believes that work should pay and enable workers to feed themselves and their families, which was the original objective of the minimum wage. Indeed, its origins go back to the creation of the Commonwealth Court of Conciliation and Arbitration, which defined it in terms of meeting "the normal needs of the average employee regarded as a human being living in a civilised community". As discussed in chapter 3, the 1907 *Harvester Case* specified that the minimum wage should enable a family of five to live in "frugal comfort". Given that the increase in the actual costs of living often exceeds official inflation, the national minimum wage (currently $18.93 an hour, $719.20 for a 38-hour week, or $37,398 per year before tax) is now insufficient to meet that goal.

According to analysis by the ACTU, the national minimum should be raised to the level of a living wage that corresponds to about 60 percent of the median wage, which currently stands at $1,320 a week. That would mean a living wage at $20.84 an hour, or $792 a week, or $41,184 per annum. So far, the ALP has not adopted this definition or undertaken a commitment to pay these amounts. Rather, a future Labor government could bring forward legislation to empower the Fair Work Commission to determine the level of the living wage and therefore how far and how fast to raise the minimum wage. These new powers would include looking ahead more than one year (as is currently the case) and giving greater importance to the relative living standards of those on the lowest incomes. Like the principle of the living wage, Labor's pledge to grant greater authority to the Fair Work Commission is also in line with the social justice tradition of the churches and its emphasis on subsidiarity – devolving decisions to the lowest level in accordance with the dignity of the person and the common good. In this case, the most appropriate level is not the state or federal government but rather an independent body.

There are three central issues, however, that Labor needs to address if it wants to bring about greater economic justice in relation to wages. One is the problem of all those workers who are not paid the minimum wage, including those in receipt of the Newstart allowance, which is in urgent need of being raised from its current level of $75 a week and $15,000 per year – less than half of the minimum wage. The second problem is the enforcement of the minimum wage where employers undercut it. Finally, there is the question of couples and families who require greater help owing to their particular needs.

The ALP should think about proposing a *family wage* that addresses this and makes good on the promise of family-friendly policies. The family wage would be paid in a manner that is appropriate to the life and responsibilities of the worker and his or her loved ones. This translates into practice a key principle of Christian social teaching – the idea of *just* prices. Politicians, business people, and trade union leaders have to recover the understanding that there are 'proper' wages or salaries to be paid for work involving different degrees of talent, labour, scope, and risk, which means that high-risk jobs or degrading ones need be better rewarded and recognised.

In addition to a family wage, other family-friendly policies that Labor could consider include allowing married couples and long-term cohabiting couples to share their tax-free allowances. That would enable them to transfer the rest of their allowance to their spouse or partner, if they themselves are not working or not using their whole allowance. It would also reduce overall tax revenue by cutting the tax bill by single-earner families with children. But this is a price worth paying for minimising the 'couple penalty' in the tax system. Linked to this is state childcare funding, which should not only go to approved childcare providers but also to parents who want to care for their children at home, especially for low-income households. Further, voluntary parenting lessons and relationship counselling should be as freely available as pre-natal classes or treatment for different forms of addiction. Such support is often best offered by intermediary institutions, including member-based societies or social enterprises that work in close coordination with local government.[18]

Labor can also pursue greater economic justice by drawing on the insights of distributism. At a time when both state socialism and market fundamentalism have failed, a renewed distributist model can offer some radical policy ideas, especially in relation to reinventing community credit unions as a concrete alternative to corporate banks. In the past, credit unions provided affordable carry-on loans for customers who were excluded from the formal banking system or simply could not afford commercial interest rates. In an age of historically low rates and a much greater variety of financial intermediaries, together with large superannuation funds that are mutual-like, there is the opportunity to be responsibly inventive. This needs to be led by people with the ideas, skills and prudence necessary. Therefore, Labor could help reinvent credit unions for the twenty-first century through a focus on unlocking capital for local and regional economies to create value, notably by way of stable meaningful jobs in small and medium-sizes businesses. The key to this is strengthening the power of members who are the major asset of credit unions – their knowledge of localities, the trust and co-operation they can bring to the economy, and above all their work and creativity. Both old and new credit unions can be re-purposed to provide larger loans to businesses based on a system of syndication between credit unions that would spread risk.

As Race Mathews has argued, risk assessment and other financial skills could be provided by professional bodies such as the Credit Union Services Corporation of Australia Limited, which is the trade association for Australian credit unions and cooperatives.[19] Within this framework, renewed credit unions could also help with business incubation and alternative forms of ownership, such as worker cooperatives or employee-shared models. Another policy idea for Labor to consider is the creation of mutualised banks with a regional and sectoral focus, constrained to lend in specific locations and economic sectors that are starved of capital. All these proposals would help to revitalise Australia's civic and economic infrastructure beneath federal and state governments as well as the increasingly globalised market.

Dignity of labour and the future of work

Work is at the heart of the ALP. The party was named after labour. Work is central to Labor's political platform and policy agenda. Some of the leading Labor MPs, especially the shadow treasurer, Jim Chalmers, are thoughtful advocates of the dignity of work in a context of insecure and precarious jobs, as well as the rapid growth in Artificial Intelligence, robotics, automation, and machine learning, which are among the greatest anxieties of Australians today.[20] As with economic justice, the ALP must return to first principles, and the social justice tradition of the churches offers some key ideas. First of all, work is a source of both income and meaning that makes us more human by drawing on, and developing, our talents and vocations. Our lives are qualitatively changed for the better when the source of income is also at least one source of meaning because we flourish more when our lives are integrated. Dignity in the workplace is a vital condition for human beings to have a share in the good life. As mentioned above, Australia's labour market is characterised by a low wage and low productivity equilibrium. Over time, a sustainable increase in wages needs labour productivity growth. The latter is linked to the skill, character, and resilience of the workforce. In turn, boosting these features requires a re-focus on vocation and the institutions involved in renewing the skills, knowledge, and craft that are necessary to adapt to changes in science and technology. A flourishing country has to rebalance public policy towards the vocational economy.

Secondly, far from being obsolete, vocation combines traditions of practice inherited from the past with transformations of skill and craft in each generation based on changes in knowledge and technology. To paraphrase Edmund Burke, an occupation without the means of some change, is without the means of its own conservation. Vocational occupations often involve apprenticeships and traineeships providing induction and a controlled vocational entry point into the labour market. Over time, occupations such as medicine, law, banking, dentistry, and accountancy were elevated in their status through legal recognition of the practices validated by the partnership between universities and professional associations and recognised by the state. Going forward, this has to happen for skilled manual labour, so that its social status is raised and its economic value more fully recognised. Such an approach requires stronger intermediary institutions because the degree of expertise and specialism cannot be known by a centralised state or be left to the unfettered market. Rather, vocational occupations have to evolve based on internal peer judgement instead of external administrative or managerial targets.

Intermediary institutions, such as trade unions or employers' associations, are vital for preserving and renewing inherited knowledge and skill. An evolving and regularly renewed inheritance can bestow status and a competitive advantage over others. At the same time as providing recognition for vocation, it is paramount to learn the lessons from the royal commissions into finance and banking, aged care, sexual abuse, and now disability services in order to avoid the abuse of trust that can come with status. One way is to devise a system of voluntary, free, guild-like institutions that include independent members who can oversee internal governance based on checks and balances. Such institutions could help to instil ethos, uphold professional standards, and support members in tangible ways, for example by assisting with the transfer of portable pensions and other entitlements when workers change employers.

Vocational institutions embody the principle of reciprocity through which mutual benefit is sustained over time through mutual contribution to a common corporate body that sustains knowledge and status. They preserve bodies of knowledge and patterns of structured co-operation by adapting to the demands of external change in terms of technology, administrative rules, and knowledge. Vocational institutions, characterised in this way, are what Aristotle called "embodiments of human meaning and purpose", an active means of integrating new knowledge with existing practice, translating information into knowledge of a specific practical kind.

Thirdly – and this matters particularly to Labor – the public recognition of vocational institutions that uphold and transmit the practices of specialised crafts and skills is vital for meaningful work because those institutions protect the internal goods of quality and expertise of specific occupations. All this boosts the capacity of the economy to innovate and to adapt to changes in the national and international context. With public support, vocational institutions serve as a source of ethical regulation and expertise, which counterbalances the reliance on external regulation. As Maurice Glasman, the founder of the Blue Labour movement in Britain,[21] argues: "the paradox is that labour market flexibility is a cause of uncompetitive production. Or, productivity is low because the status of labour is weak".[22] Another way of saying this is to suggest that productive and resilient economies require non-market civic institutions that embed markets into relations going beyond instrumental function towards a wider social purpose. Such institutions uphold standards of excellence and ethos through work licenses that permit and regulate the practice of a craft, trade, or profession, often by way of apprenticeships and other forms of vocational entry into the labour market.

Fourthly, a vocational economy involves the practice of virtue. This does not entail the moralistic sense of telling people how to behave. Rather, virtue is what the Catholic philosopher Alasdair MacIntyre defines as "an acquired human quality – the possession and exercise of which ends to enable us to achieve those goods which are internal to practices".[23] Economic virtue pursues good practice as defined by a vocation or profession based on craft, skill, honesty, courage, and solidarity, all of which are necessary for innovation and competitiveness. Examples include stronger rights to collective bargaining and worker representation on company boards and their remuneration committees, as well as the co-determination of pensions by capital and labour. This is the case in the social market economy of Germany, which is among the most competitive countries in the world. Its model grew out of Catholic social teaching and Christian democracy, and it is characterised by the plural governance of non-pecuniary institutions that uphold and embody a virtue that is irreducible to state or market definitions.

As Germany and other countries with an important vocational economy attest, economic success depends on a balance between inherited knowledge and practice, on the one hand, and technological advancement and new knowledge, on the other. Innovation is not and should not be primarily about replacing the old with the new, but rather renewing and extending good practice and re-ordering received ideas in different combinations in order to form novel patterns based on existing practice. Innovative economies pursue perfectibility within existing institutions, not perfection *ex nihilo*. New technologies linked to automation, robotics, or Artificial Intelligence require existing expertise to assimilate and adapt them to production processes. Otherwise innovation is destroying instead of creating value.[24] For instance, a proper defence of the labour interest by the ALP should include creating new public trusts for the pooling of technological knowledge to replace the current patenting system in which at present the dominant patent model favours large private corporations over smaller, more innovative, and social enterprise. Such a scheme would also involve fostering workplace innovation through continuous on-the-job learning and through life training, better skills use, innovation around teamwork, and a culture of trust and cooperation rather than compliance.

Fifthly, vocational institutions are vital for preserving and renewing the skills that enable workers to turn new ideas and technologies into real value – not just abstract financial wealth. They promote good practice, or virtue, within the economy by defending persons and knowledge against commodification and by linking production to social purpose.[25] In Germany, parts of France, and northern Italy, for example, there are strong artisanal sectors in which vocational institutions oversee labour market qualifications and licences, and thereby constrain competition away from a race to the bottom. The state has a key role in creating the space for vocational and professional self-association, but also through active support for colleges and artisan guilds, whether via annual funding or based on an endowment. There is much to learn from this institutional ecology that preserves non-contractual organisations that uphold values and the internal goods of economic activities – not just the extraction of financial profit.

From the perspective of the ALP, the building of a stronger vocational economy is in line with the party's best traditions and also a way of reaching out to disaffected working families. Championing the living wage is only a starting point, and Labor should also strengthen the status of vocation for labour market entry as a form of ethical self-regulation of crafts and professions under the broad aegis of the state. Vocational colleges, guilds, and universities that uphold ethos and excellence are institutional pillars for a richer economy which generates values and shared prosperity. These institutions mediate between the extreme rationality of technocratic administration on the one hand and the irrational exuberance of unfettered markets and the herd behaviour we observe in the most financialised parts of the world economy. Some of the policy arguments that follow from this analysis include the following:

1. Cognitive and transferable knowledge needs to be balanced by vocational and craft-specific knowledge, which requires a transformation of education and training;

2. The expansion of universities needs to be balanced by vocational and technical colleges, co-funded and supported by the state, employers, and trade unions;

3. There could be vocational and technical pathways in secondary schools that lead to the apprenticeships in partnership with vocational and technical colleges;

4. New national colleges could be established as democratic organisations that ethically regulate the manual trades that are now deregulated;

5. Vocation is given equal legal recognition as for the professions.

Concrete policies that embody these principles include, first of all, bringing Technical and Further Education (TAFE) as well as vocational education under a single federal umbrella in order to create a consistent national system of accredited courses. Secondly, Labor should launch a rethink about more hybrid courses and institutions that can fuse academic, vocational, and technical education for subjects such as engineering and medicine, but also caring (as suggested below in greater detail). One important effect would be to help raise over time not only the incomes of such occupations but also their social recognition. Thirdly, both the state and the market have to provide many more apprenticeships, either separately or in partnership. As Nick Dyrenfurth suggests, "employer groups and local chambers of commerce can play a critical role, acting as a conduit between government, TAFE and vocational education providers, unions and business".[26]

Connected with the centrality of vocation is the production of value, which by far exceeds financial value and extends to labour value, including human creativity and ingenuity. While certain thriving sectors are part of the 'knowledge economy' with its emphasis on general, transferable skills, other sectors that are growing in importance involve vocational and manual skills – care being a particularly important area. The numbers of carers, including those working in aged-care, childcare or disability care, has been one of the fast-growing occupations in Australia for the last decade, with an increase of 170,000 workers from 2006 to 2016 and a total workforce of almost half a million workers. This has gone hand in hand with a booming healthcare sector, which has grown at twice the pace of the rest of the labour market. But for many workers pay is only marginally higher than the minimum wage and falls well short of a living wage.

Besides higher pay and better working conditions, greater equality for women – who are the overwhelming majority among care workers – is needed. The care sector also requires much more strategic support. For example, higher life expectancy is increasing the demand for care of older people who are often lonely and frail. The desire of many older people to remain in their own homes as they age requires greater provision of aged-care services in local communities rather than residential care homes. There are also growing needs in relation to childcare and disability care. The ALP has a proud record of establishing the National Disability Insurance Scheme (NDIS), of which Bill Shorten was an early proponent as Parliamentary Secretary for Disabilities and Children's Services in the first Rudd government. Public funding models for aged care and childcare have formalised many of the jobs, and demand is growing exponentially, with the Department of Employment, Skills, Small and Family Business predicting that until 2025, aged and disability care workers will grow by a further 40 percent and the childcare workforce by 18 percent. Among the key challenges are funding and adequate resources, the delivery of personal care, the standards of caring, and the working conditions for carers.

The ALP could address some of these issues by creating an Australian college for aged care – Aged Care Australia (ACA). The basic idea is to establish ACA as a civil society organisation that is democratically governed and which provides both ethical and professional regulation for a vocational profession that lacks economic reward and social recognition. ACA would be both a professional body – concerned with the education and training of carers and caring standards – and a trade union. Members would be drawn from the public, the private, and the voluntary sectors. Retired carers and those training to be carers would also be offered membership. ACA would offer its members free confidential advice and support on employment conditions, career development, immigration, welfare, and other matters. On governance, various options are available. The old fault lines of the interests of the producer versus the consumers, those to be trained and upskilled, and the interests of society as a whole need balancing. I suggest that ACA could be governed by an elected Council whose president sits on the board – headed by a chief executive and general secretary who is responsible for its management. ACA's charter could emphasise two aspects in particular: (1) the centrality of formation – formation of ethos, character, and vocational skills; (2) a balance of interests between carers and their employers – in relation to pay, terms and conditions of employment, and pensions.

The key to ACA is to elevate the status of aged care as a vocation through the legal recognition of specific practices. Vocation involves three important aspects: first, a person's *calling*, in the sense of finding meaning and fulfilment in one's labour, which is specific to a person and not transferrable; second, a balance between tradition and innovation; third, the importance of virtue, including honesty, courage and solidarity.

The ACA could valorise those traditions of practice inherited from the past and transformed in each generation by changes in knowledge, technology, and practice. It would recognise the importance of apprenticeship, induction, and acculturation combined with greater control over vocational labour market entry. As a common institution that sustains knowledge and status, the work of the ACA would be based on the principle of reciprocity – relationships of give-and-take that help to ensure that members fulfil their obligation to contribute and in turn to earn their just reward. As a vocational institution configured in this way, ACA would be what Aristotle called an "embodiment of human meaning and purpose". In concrete terms, this means integrating new knowledge with existing practice and translating novel information into knowledge of a specific practical kind or skill. In turn, this would involve a partnership with universities, other related professional associations in the healthcare sector and local, state, or federal government. Other roles of the ACA could include:

1. training of carers based on high-quality research and the exchange of good practice with similar institutions in other countries; and,

2. working with government and other bodies to shape and implement policy that improves the quality of aged care (such as providing advice to legislators and regulators, campaigning on pay and employment conditions for carers).

Against what I have written are two points. Firstly, that a Burkean perspective might seek reform utilising existing institutions rather than something *ab initio*. Secondly, some of the actors required to make the ACA work may be unsympathetic or hostile. Such might include existing administrators, unions, and operators seeking to protect their turf. There is nothing as achingly hard than a reform that begs consideration of large-scale change. Learning from existing operations and practices needs to be part of the story. I cannot exhaustively sketch a game plan for realisation. All I can offer is a plea: 'what is better?' 'What needs doing to meet the challenge?' Can we at least do that?

In short, boosting vocation makes eminent economic and ethical sense. It diversifies the knowledge and skills basis and sustains a job-creating innovative economy, while its beneficiaries can have occupations that earn a decent income and provide meaning. Partnerships between public, private, and third-sector institutions help to make a contribution to the community and the country – on which Australia's prosperity and cohesion depends.

Meritocracy

A more balanced economy matters for other reasons too. As the French political economist Thomas Piketty argues, the new tendency to extreme concentration of wealth combines the resurgent importance of inherited wealth in a period of low growth with the newly excessive salaries and bonuses encouraged by a climate of what he calls "meritocratic extremism".[27] Extremist meritocracy, exacerbated into a kind of generalised Hollywood star-cult, now means that a culture allegedly based on ability awards 'extreme' ability extremely much. Meanwhile, high salaries are taken to be the automatic result of education and applied talent in a self-confirming circle. The idea that the prevailing system rewards talent and hard work induces the winners to view their success as their own achievement and as confirmation of their own virtue – which leads to self-righteousness and an attitude of contempt towards those who are less successful and fortunate than them.

In reality, international comparisons show that the much higher disparities of income in Anglo-Saxon countries can by no means be correlated with factors of merit. The Anglosphere is in the grip of a dangerous economic and cultural fantasy because the predominant system rewards greed that corrodes the culture on which true merit rests. A growing part of the metropolitan meritocracy is little more than the wealthy few who enjoy greater access to education and the power to grant legitimacy to their own modes of culture, while profitably palming off the populace with a debased mass variety. In either case, culture gets commodified and is thereby divorced from substantial social action and virtue. Another way of saying this is to suggest that the reigning ideology of 'meritocratic extremism' confuses merit with monetary return and even skill in monetary manipulation with the luck of the draw.

Citing Michael Young who coined the term 'meritocracy', Piketty acknowledges that modern meritocrats tend to assume yet more cultural control in consequence of their social position than did the nineteenth-century gentry described so vividly in the work of Jane Austen and Honoré de Balzac.[28] They despise much more the indigent and poor, since this status is now regarded as 'their fault', rather than as an accident of birth.[29] It is therefore not surprising that Western countries, Australia included, are witnessing a popular revulsion against the excesses of meritocratic extremism. This is threefold: first, the 'success' culture that operates at the expense of most people; secondly, the amoral and narrow criteria that define this success; thirdly, a cosmopolitan contempt for an embedded sense of belonging as well as a yearning for meaning and purpose. The meritocratic metropolitan elites fail to understand that the anti-establishment insurgents are a consequence, not the cause, of the failure of economic liberalism and some of its social effects.

Like other social-democratic parties, the ALP needs to question its over-devotion to technocratic politics whereby the state tinkers with private profits in order to secure material interests – a combination of trickle-down wealth qualified by top-down redistribution. Instead, Labor needs to revisit its legacy of ethical commitment and its protection of workers and their ways of life, as opposed to the promotion of mass commercial culture which does not even serve the true needs of the middle class. An alternative approach would therefore combine a search for restored community with the search for more holistic fulfilment in work. This can be linked to the search for the combining of work with the needs of family and community, including a focus on the mutual obligations that are ignored by liberal concerns about equal opportunities and free choice. Though important, these objectives often operate at the expense of reciprocal relationships and shared prosperity.

An alternative approach would also *not* give absolute priority to the mantra of social mobility because the latter is predicated on the idea of winners and losers, with the former reaping disproportionate benefits while the latter are compensated by the state or left to fend for themselves. Even if social mobility has a certain validity and importance within a specific range, it nevertheless needs to be transformed by a wider effort to raise the status of vocations and professions currently not considered as a success and hence not properly rewarded or socially recognised. Finally, Labor should oppose the idea of a race to the bottom in terms of professional standards and individual behaviour, like cutting corners or the motto 'greed is good'. A more just perspective is to try to broker cooperation where there are conflicts of interest and to bring people together in a nobler and more benign rivalry over honourable achievement and excellent performance.

In practical terms, the ALP needs to champion whole families and communities in need of nurturing. It has been demonstrated in practice that only a holistic tackling of aspects of a deprived local community's life, including the initially gratuitous distribution of owned assets, resources, and responsibilities, can make any effective and long-term difference. By the same token, Labor wants to bring about a shift in focus away from a reactive approach that mostly deals with the effects of problems (e.g., unemployment and ill-health) and towards a proactive stance that tackles the root causes by adopting a strategy of early intervention. For example, teaching underprivileged parents to read with their children has been shown to be decisive.

Further examples include childcare for those couples where both spouses or partners want to work. The ALP could also champion policies that help those parents wishing to stay home for reasons of childcare, for example by extending paid parental leave to eighteen months or two years. Other policies include measures aimed at protecting the ways of life of workers, through limits on untargeted economic immigration and a better integration of migrants. To achieve thus, Labor needs to become a party that understands its core voters and selects candidates who represent them.

Patriotism and national community

Beyond the economy and questions of social mobility, Labor must reclaim patriotism from the Liberals if it is to win back some of its traditional supporters. The populist insurgency sweeping the West is fuelled by a popular backlash against the socio-cultural effects of immigration and free trade. These are not only economic issues linked to pressure on wages and job losses, but also touch on questions of self-worth and mutual recognition. Do politicians and businesses value cheap labour and cheap goods or services more than respect for their fellow citizens? Arguments about those questions need to be won. The experience, or threat, of dispossession and humiliation feeds a sense of betrayal that either leads to disaffection or alienation from politics, or else finds a profoundly problematic expression – support for political extremes, combined with nationalism, xenophobia, and even racism. A simple reassertion of social progressivism around equality, diversity, and inclusivity risks making a polarised politics worse by not addressing fundamental questions of nationhood and citizenship.[30] What are the boundaries of a shared political community? How do we recognise the importance of borders for many citizens while also being generous to 'strangers in our midst'? Do we owe particular obligations to our fellow citizens that we do not owe to the citizens of other countries? What, if any, is the moral difference between refugees and economic migrants?

Faced with the support for the populist uprising of One Nation and the United Australia Party, Labor cannot afford to leave these questions to the Liberal Party and its claim to represent 'quiet Australians'. Rather, the ALP needs to renew democratic debate by speaking out on big issues that many people care about, including complex moral and cultural questions. In recent years, Labor is seen on the side of liberal multiculturalism. Of course, there are many reasons to defend Australia's multicultural model, especially in the aftermath of ending the White Australia Policy. But as Chapter 3 suggested, patriotism is also central to the ALP's history and philosophy. Therefore, Labor can offer two things that the Liberals will struggle to match – the recognition of Aboriginal and Torres Strait Islander people and a patriotic vision for all Australians beyond class, colour, or creed.

The Labor Party's record of fighting for a fuller recognition of the rights of Aboriginal and Torres Strait Islander people can be extended. That record includes Gough Whitlam's creation of the department for Aboriginal affairs in 1972, Paul Keating's historic Redfern speech in 1993, Kim Beazley's motion of apology and reconciliation in 1997 (following the publication of the *Bringing Them Home* report), and Kevin Rudd's full apology to the Stolen Generation in 2008. Binding together the actions of these three Labor prime ministers is the acknowledgement of guilt on the part of the Australian state for the injustices suffered by the country's Indigenous people and some measures to restore land rights and foster self-determination. Whitlam personally gave land title deeds to the Gurindji people in 1975, a moment captured forever when Aboriginal photographer Merv Bishop took his famous photo of Gough pouring a fistful of soil into Vincent Lingiari's hand. In addition, the government led by Whitlam set up the Aboriginal Loans Commission, the Aboriginal Land Fund Commission and the National Aboriginal Consultative Committee, the first national advisory structure for Indigenous people to select their own representatives and to advise the federal government.

Keating showed how restoring care and dignity to the Aboriginal and Torres Strait Islander peoples is inextricably intertwined with the integrity of all Australians: the point of his Redfern Speech was "to bring the dispossessed out of the shadows, to recognise that they are part of us, and that we cannot give Indigenous Australians up without giving up many of our own most deeply held values, much of our own identity – and our own humanity".[31] This goes to the heart of Labor's purpose – restoring dignity to those stripped of it and giving them a share of the good life. This noble ambition required a full apology for the appalling injustice of past deeds, which is why Beazley's motion was so important and Rudd's speech so crucial: "For the pain, suffering and hurt of these Stolen Generations, their descendants and for their families left behind, we say sorry".[32] Beazley and Rudd's empathy, together with Keating's accentuation of the shared destiny of all Australians, laid the foundations for national reconciliation.

But Australia still has not recognised the full significance of Aboriginal and Torres Strait Islander peoples by giving them proper recognition in the country's Constitution or a direct voice and power in public affairs, or tackling their disproportionate disadvantages relative to the rest of the population. Just as the recognition and proper treatment of First Australians was little more than a side issue in the 2019 elections, so too the acknowledgement of country at the beginning of events or speeches is but an incomplete recognition – a formulaic declaration that risks becoming ritualistic and devoid of enduring meaning. Moreover, the response to the Uluru Statement by both the Liberal Party and the ALP was insufficient, given that this statement reflects a national Indigenous consensus on constitutional recognition which grew out of a convention of 250 Aboriginal and Torres Strait Islander delegates. It called for the creation of a First Nations Voice enshrined in the Constitution and the establishment of a Makarrata Commission to oversee a process of truth and reconciliation between First Australians and governments at both federal and state level. What is missing is leadership to build on this broad-based community consensus in order to create bi-partisan support for political action.

Prime Minister Morrison vowed to "govern for all Australians". But much of his party will likely resist constitutional recognition in line with the Uluru Statement on the grounds that a treaty or, in Yolngu language, 'makarrata', is supposedly divisive and an expression of identity politics. Under Albanese's leadership, Labor can appeal to the greater national good while also acting in accordance with the Constitution and political culture. The ALP should carefully consider the set of proposals as developed by the PM Glynn Institute at the Australian Catholic University and the organisation Uphold & Recognise.[33] The mark of their proposals is to combine a recognition of Australian nationhood, which reflects the Indigenous heritage, British-inspired institutions, and the achievements of multiculturalism, with a set of practical reforms that give Indigenous communities and their representatives a voice and power to shape public affairs. This could take the form of a declaration outside Australia's Constitution, coupled with a series of new laws and institutional arrangements, which would include modest constitutional amendments. This approach avoids two principal obstacles: one is a fundamental constitutional amendment, which would introduce legal uncertainty, and the other is a third chamber, which would destabilise the existing parliamentary structure.

A declaration of recognition outside the Constitution has the double advantage of not being constrained by legal language and of not transferring power from Parliament to the High Court. Instead, such a declaration can express Australia's nationhood and thereby provide the symbolism of national unity, which creates the spaces for real legal and political reforms. In this manner, these proposals fuse symbolic with substantive recognition. Of course, the process of drafting this declaration will be contentious and fraught with difficulties, but drawing on existing statements (such as 1998 Australian Declaration towards Reconciliation, the 2008 national apology, and the Australian Parliament's *Aboriginal and Torres Strait Islander Peoples Recognition Act 2013*), the declaration would likely incorporate eight themes:

1. Recognition of the traditional owners of the land that comprises modern Australia;
2. Acknowledgment of their ongoing connection to their traditional lands and waters;
3. Affirmation of the heritage, culture, and languages of Australia's Indigenous peoples;
4. Reverence for the oldest continuing civilisation in the world;
5. Reflection about the past mistreatment of Indigenous peoples;
6. Recitation of the values shared by Australian citizens;

7. Recognition of the institutions central to Australian government; and

8. Recognition of the contribution of waves of immigration to a multicultural society.[34]

A declaration along those lines would be the culmination of a process of reform that focuses on practical legal and political changes, including creating a mechanism whereby First Australians can have their voices heard by using Parliament's current powers, rather than modifying existing ones or creating new ones. For example, a constitutional obligation to consult Indigenous People and consider the advice of their delegates must be appropriately limited to proposed laws specifically concerning Indigenous affairs, such as health, education or housing. This model would require both Parliament and the Executive branch of government to set up a meaningful dialogue with the constitutionally mandated Indigenous voice(s), either by way of local entities or a national body. In each case what is needed are links from the local via the regional to the national level, and a proper mechanism for recognising which local Indigenous entity speaks for which group and how they can be federated into a national voice – such as through the form of an advisory council. Central to the success of such an approach is the continual engagement with Indigenous views throughout the policy and law-making process in order to give these reforms their proper democratic legitimacy within Australia's constitutional settlement.

Above all, Labor must listen to Indigenous Australia and represent its interests. By developing the proposals put forward by the PM Glynn Institute and Uphold & Recognise, the ALP would once again be true to its own legacy of being the national popular party that pursues the common good of all Australians.

In terms of patriotism and nation-building, another interesting policy idea that could help Labor to regain popular trust is to establish a National Civic Service (NCS). Such a scheme would aim to nurture the practice of democratic citizenship, especially obligations as a citizen to oneself and to others in society. Starting with 16-25 year-old Australians, the NCS would be compulsory and run for between six months and one year – followed by a life-cycle of much shorter periods of civic engagement. Over time, the scheme could be extended to people of all ages. In some respects, it is modelled on those who are reservists in the army and train periodically, with the difference that the NCS is obligatory – unless people have done military service. The NCS is neither a programme to enhance employability nor a nation-wide forum for volunteering. Such models are valuable in their own right, but they do not by themselves promote democratic participation. Faced with the growing popular distrust of politics and public institutions, especially disaffection with the mainstream political parties, it is imperative to foster stronger democratic participation in the national civic community through building bridges between estranged interests and sections of society that are divided from one another.

Examples of potential NCS activities include community work in schools, children's centres, and care homes, as well as housing or park projects, or support for emergency services such as flood defences and bushfires. Through a mix of discipline and encouragement, people would learn how to forge social ties, trust, and cooperation where these are missing. One of the main objectives is to create an 'encounter culture' in which citizens of all ages and backgrounds meet and build relationships around shared interests – becoming more-informed citizens, providing help based on their specific talents and vocations, and developing practical 'life' skills in an age in which traditional socialisation and rites of passage are lacking. Many people – young and old, urban and rural, Indigenous or immigrant – grow up with a thin conception of citizenship and are sceptical about the meaning of society or how it might relate to them and people like themselves.

Young people aged 16-25 doing the NCS would be paid the national minimum wage to work on projects to support children, the sick and elderly, the environment, and international development. Daily visits to help with household tasks such as shopping, cooking, cleaning, or gardening could keep thousands of elderly people out of care homes. Groups of mentors, readings coaches, classroom assistants, sport aides, and after-school carers could help with childcare and youth support, which would assist both schools and families with two breadwinners. Working on environmental projects in agriculture, forestry, or fishing communities would provide help to sectors that sometimes struggle to attract the necessary workforce while also injecting a stronger ecological spirit. And building wells and schools abroad would provide real help in developing countries. For those who struggle to make the transition from adolescence to adulthood and those who lack educational or employment opportunities, such a scheme would go some way towards addressing social needs that are not met by the state or the market – offering young people institutional structures, rites of passage, and thereby an important measure of social esteem. For adults who would start doing the NCS in its second phase, it would reaffirm their commitment to citizenship and the nation in concrete ways. Employer support and participation would make a valuable contribution to the NCS.

Along with compulsory voting, an obligatory NCS would increase democratic participation in wider society anchored in a strong sense of citizenship and mutual civic obligations. The effects of rampant individualism over the past forty years or so have produced nearly three generations of citizens whose passage to adulthood has been more individualised and whose social identity is more atomised. Routes into the labour markets are less vocational, while academic education puts the onus on general transferable skills that do not speak to particular talents. Early marriage and clear gender roles are in sharp decline, which offers opportunities based on individual rights and freedoms, but these phenomena can also lead to higher levels of selfishness and greed with adverse effects on individuals and society as a whole – a lack of empathy and compassion.

At the same time, we need such social and civic virtues. The changes in the economy away from industry and manufacturing towards services and automation shift the emphasis onto social skills – working with people from very diverse backgrounds, self-discipline, and sympathy with others we do not know well. Both generation X and the millennials are "freedom's orphans" – people who are at once more interdependent and more atomised: as Michael Sandel wrote in 1984, "in our public life we are more entangled, but less attached, than ever before".[35] The primary goal of instituting a compulsory NCS would be to offer multiple activities aimed at character and bridge-building between individuals and groups lacking social ties and civic virtue – courage, patience, generosity, loyalty, and lived fraternity. It would support a new age of obligations, matching the re-moralisation of the economy and the polity with a vision of society based on the common good. On the NCS, a practical difficulty is the cost, time, and effort to ensure the right people are engaged, the appropriate skills cultivated, the trainers attuned to what needs doing, with lessons learnt being part of the on-going experience. I have suggested a very large idea, actually something similar to what Labor Prime Minister Andrew Fisher advocated over 110 years ago. Something this ambitious needs trialling, growing, and learning from. This is a distinctly Labor proposal because it translates the principle of progressive patriotism into transformative practices of community and nation-building based on a sense of collective agency.

Foreign Policy

In recent years, Labor framed its foreign policy on three pillars: the American-Australian alliance, Australia's relationships in the Indo-Pacific, and the country's multilateral engagement in the world. Relations with the three great powers to our north – China, Japan, and Indonesia – are central. The continuing rise of India is another relationship worth fostering and deepening. A complementary approach, which partly converges and partly diverges with this thinking, draws on the BBC Reith Lectures in the early 1950s by Oliver Frank, in which he developed a notion first popularised by Winston Churchill about Britain being at the centre of the "three interlocking circles" of the United States, Europe, and the Commonwealth. Applied to Australia, this conception means that the country is central to the Western alliance, the wider Indo-Pacific region including the focus on island countries, and the association of the Commonwealth. The advantage of interlocking circles is that they capture the overlap of the three areas and provide common ground rather than privileging one pillar over another; all pillars are important.

The election of Donald Trump and his strange attitudes to allies and alliances brings into stark relief that there are no permanent, absolutely reliable allies, whatever be the shared values between peoples. Australia needs to be more self-reliant without abrogating our existing treaty relationships. This is important not least because of Australia's complacent over-reliance on the United States. It is true that since the Atlantic Charter of 1941 and the government led by John Curtin, Australia is proudly part of the Anglophone alliance that includes the United States, the United Kingdom, Canada, and New Zealand. This alliance is the backbone of Australia's national security and international engagement. Australians were both architects and advocates of this alliance from the time of Curtin as war leader and Evatt as Foreign Minister (and as President of the United Nations' General Assembly) all the way to Gareth Evans and his contribution to the United Nations peace plan for Cambodia and his role in establishing the Asia-Pacific Economic Cooperation (APEC). More recently, whether in the war on terror or in relation to foreign powers such as China and Russia, the Anglophone alliance and the 'five eyes' partnership is not confined to signals intelligence but comprises defence intelligence, human intelligence, and geospatial intelligence. That makes Australia an important player.

But dependence on the United States or previously on the United Kingdom can come at a price, if independent thinking about Australia's interests is not part of the foreign policy nomenclature. Even pro-American Labor leaders such as Curtin, Hawke, and Keating acknowledge the need to build other coalitions and relationships, especially with the countries in Australia's neighbourhood, and the members of the Commonwealth. On the latter for example, Hawke not only supported Malcolm Fraser's joint leadership of the Commonwealth Eminent Persons Group and its mission to South Africa in 1986 but also applied pressure to the apartheid system through other Commonwealth mechanisms.

Under Keating, Australia built important international partnerships. As he saw it, Australia had historically sought protection *from* Asia, whereas the contemporary challenge is to see Australia's interests advanced through security *in* Asia. Among the great achievements of the Hawke-Keating era was the creation of APEC which, under Keating, became a leaders' forum. Labor defends Australia's interests by seeking to be an economic partner of China and a bridge to an understanding of that country and the West. This is a key role in the context of a Western pivot away from a focus on the Atlantic towards a focus on the Asia-Pacific region. As Kim Beazley argues,

> By the time I got to Washington in 2010 [as Australia's Ambassador], Asia was the focal point of American interest – indeed, shortly after I arrived the US 'rebalance' was announced. So the American alliance with Australia ceased to be a relationship with a backwater and we became more central to the US. At the same time, as our region developed greater economic and military capabilities, America's overall engagement in the region became much more important to us.[36]

The security alliance with the United States need not oblige Australia to follow every whim and caprice of an American administration. It is important always to advance the country's national objectives in an increasingly interdependent world. At a time when Australia lacks a dynamic foreign policy, the ALP can fill that gap.

The radical alternative in line with Australia's tradition of constitutionalism is therefore that of re-thinking the country's global role at the heart of those circles with whom the country interacts, starting with the island nations in the wider Indo-Pacific region. Most notably, Australia's sphere of influence includes Indonesia, Japan, and New Zealand, anchored in institutions that reflect commonly agreed principles and enforced rules, but above all a commitment to a shared purpose of peace, prosperity, and partnership based on joint interests. Such an approach reflects Labor's governing philosophy of linking foreign policy and national defence and security to radical reform and social purpose at home. The focus on island nations makes sense in relation to geo-political, geo-cultural, and increasingly geo-ecological considerations. Whether in the context of the rising rivalry between the United States and China, or the importance of social and cultural ties beyond politics and commerce, or the threat posed by environmental devastation, the island nations across the Indo-Pacific region have a key role to play as mediators and pioneers in collective action. No single island power will be able to dominate the others, and all reject domination from external hegemons. The principle of non-domination is not merely negative but instead translates into practices of reciprocity – the reciprocal recognition of rights, obligations, and substantive interests. By putting respect and cooperation at the heart of the Indo-Pacific region, Australia can help to give multilateral action meaning and substance.

Collective action anchored in shared interests and the pursuit of the common good are hallmarks of Labor's approach to both domestic and international politics. The ALP's best tradition is to combine a national, popular patriotism with a generous yet realistic internationalism, which means to put good citizenship, democracy, and making people partners in power before profit, domination, or cosmopolitan abstraction from nationhood. These principled practices should also characterise the Commonwealth based on the historic ties of common law, language, history, and culture. Australia, together with India, the United Kingdom, and Canada, has a special responsibility to renew Commonwealth cooperation and turn it into a global partnership that can mediate between the United States and

China, but also bring Europe (and over time Russia) into a meaningful dialogue of civilisations and cultures. A Labor Party committed to patriotism and internationalism alike cannot lose sight of such noble ambitions.

Conclusion
The purpose of power

Graham Freudenberg, speechwriter to various Labor leaders, once characterised his beloved party: "The Australian Labor Party was born with a sense of history. That sense of its past has always been, and remains, one of its great sources of strength and its confidence about its future".[1] As it learns the lessons of its defeat in 2019, the party needs to remember that Labor only gains and retains power when it represents both the labour interest and the national interest. That means representing the millions of Australians who care about family, work, community, and country. To win a majority and govern in the national interest, the ALP has to reform its party organisation, political culture, and policy offer, in a way that is underpinned by a working philosophy.

What is the party's purpose? What are the principles anchored in the values and beliefs of the labour movement that animate the ALP?

My answer to those challenges is to say that at the heart of Labor's ethical outlook lies the idea of rewarding work as a contribution to shared prosperity and a secure meaningful life. Giving people a "share in those things that make life worth living" rests on a conception of justice that exceeds utility and individual rights in the direction of the common good. It involves ordering relationships in a way that holds in balance individual fulfilment and mutual flourishing, based on the dignity and equality of all people. Promoting the common good resonates strongly with the ALP's founding traditions, such as the trade union movement, Christian and faith-based traditions, including Catholic social teaching, Nonconformist religions, and intermediary institutions of working-class self-help. Partly because of their shared roots in Australia's Judeo-Christian heritage and partly because of a joint belief in the centrality of social justice, renewing all these traditions is relevant for the ALP's approach to the main issues of public policy – equality, secure jobs, workplace participation, automation, healthcare, social care, education, climate change, and the rise of new foreign powers.

In this book, I have tried to develop three arguments. First of all, a strong ethical purpose is vital to the party's future as it provides a compass for politics and policy in an age of upheaval. Amid the fragmentation of the centre ground and the rise of fringe extremes, the ALP is not immune from fundamental realignments in the contemporary political culture. Declining vote-shares of the two major parties and their mutation from mass movements into small elite-dominated organisations have led to popular detachment from the professional political class. This comes at a time of alienation and anger, when swathes of the ALP's former core electorate of blue-collar workers have abandoned the party. Labor's purpose and philosophical outlook is central to winning elections and brokering a politics of national renewal. The party's commitment to the common good and the good life are critical to addressing questions confronting each political generation: What is Labor for? Can we identify its character or sentiment? What are its organising principles for government? How will it devise and enact a policy agenda that reflects its original mission of democratising politics and 'civilising capitalism' (in that judicious phrase of Bede Nairn)?[2]

My answer to those questions is my second point. The ALP is only true to its history of being a broad church when its governing philosophy and values reflect those of a majority of Australian people: hard work, family and friends, the communities and localities people inhabit, and more generally a sense of justice and decency – all of which underpins the fair go. In this sense, the ALP is a party *of* the left but not exclusively *on* the left. Labor's historic purpose of empowering excluded voices and reconciling estranged interests requires reintegrating exiled traditions. Far from being nostalgic or reactionary, remembering the past is vital for the ALP as it reclaims the fair go from the Liberals and wins over the 'quiet Australians'.

My third argument is Labor must learn the hard lessons of its defeat in 2019, notably privileging progressive positions at the expense of a majority politics. Labor's contemporary language of social liberalism plays well in Sydney's and Melbourne's metropolitan parts where the party competes against the Greens, but it fails to resonate with Australians in suburban and rural regions – including those Queensland seats the ALP needed to win in order to be the largest party. Labor has to listen to the people who do not presently trust it and engage in a genuine contest of ideas. Debate is vital.

The formation of ideas is the lifeblood of political parties. Some of the ALP's present policies are the product of abstraction from the everyday existence of ordinary citizens. Unrooted in the experience of real people, such ideas can be toxic. For example, notions of diversity and inclusivity that privilege cultural liberation over economic justice, individualised identity over common culture, and private choice over shared agency. Leadership requires assessment of unintended consequences and the management of competing positions. The tension can be invigorating. But mismanaged and poorly articulated (usually a sign of confusion), they produce outcomes and practices that are remote and disconnected from the lives of those people the Labor Party purports to represent.

One implication of these three arguments is that the Labor Party never was – and never should be – an exclusively progressive party in the contemporary sense of socio-economic liberalisation. Rather, the ethos of the ALP can best be understood as a paradoxical combination of radical and small-c conservative values in a Burkean sense: tackling injustice in the economy and renewing political institutions, while also conserving tradition and society. This outlook is key to a rich political and policy framework that can help the ALP not just to win office, but also to marry power with purpose – brokering a politics of the common good based on shared interests and a balance between individual rights and mutual obligations.

Another implication concerns the future of social democracy more generally. In the 2010s social democratic parties across the West lost elections and were ejected from power. Many of them struggle to understand the forces of economic and social insecurity that undermine a sense of national identity and settled ways of life.

The centre-left fails to recognise that many ordinary people are less interested in free choice, open borders, and cosmopolitanism. They value work, family, inherited culture, and a measure of social stability. Social democracy's historic concern was with such Burkean themes anchored in a conception of the good life. If social-democratic parties lack an animating purpose today, it is because they focus too much on individual rights and collective utility. They have abandoned ethical thinking and are not even trying to re-moralise politics.

In an interview with the *New Statesman's* editor, Jason Cowley, just before the Brexit referendum in June 2016, the political philosopher Michael Sandel diagnosed the crisis of the centre-left.[3] He began by reflecting on the movement for Brexit and for Trump as expressions of profound frustration with mainstream politicians, parties, and the void at the centre of politics. Above all, the growing support for the radical right and the cranky left reflects the powerlessness of most people to control the forces governing their lives. This fuels the rage against a system that is seen as rigged against ordinary folk. Central to our age of anger is a political economy of low wages, the unholy alliance of big business with big government, humiliation, and a lack of mutual recognition. The dignity of labour has been eroded by globalisation. Australian Labor's defeat in 2019 shows that the left struggles to offer a constructive alternative to the mainstream model – which is in crisis.

Sandel's central argument is that the slide of social democracy into minority politics is the consequence of a loss of moral and civic vision. In the era of post-war reconstruction and then onwards, the left's animating purpose translated into a new settlement based on full employment, public investment, and the welfare state. The 'third way' of Bill Clinton and Tony Blair sought to bend Reagan and Thatcher's neo-liberal model to progressive ends, but their vision of 'capitalism with a human face' never questioned the liberal economic foundations of globalisation. All the talk of building a 'new centre' ended in failure as social democrats did not bring about a lasting renewal of ideas and political organisation. Missing this historic chance has beset the centre-left ever since, especially after the global financial crash in 2008-09. By that time, social democracy had become increasingly indistinguishable from the centre-right – as exemplified the austerity-lite strategy of the British Labour Party in 2015 that cost it the election that year.

Moreover, social democracy has abandoned its traditional working class base and become remote, technocratic, and managerial – representing a new professional class that is predominantly urban, metropolitan, and liberal-progressivist. As the liberal centre collapsed, the ensuing void is being filled by the radical right that opposes immigration and a resentful left that wants to abolish the market. Sandel's final point was the most decisive. To survive and once again thrive, the centre-left

> has to return to its roots in a kind of moral and civil critique of the excesses of capitalism. At the level of public philosophy or ideology it has to work out a conception of a just society, it has to work out a conception of the common good, it has to work out a conception of moral and civic education as it relates to democracy and empowerment. That is a big project and it hasn't yet been realised by any contemporary social-democratic party.[4]

Australian Labor needs to renew its ethical thinking anchored in the common good. The party requires a public political philosophy that focuses not only on fiscal transfer but more on devolving power and giving people a share in the country's prosperity – less on the state that does things to citizens, and more on a state that promotes human creativity and nurtures agency where people live. The party's paradoxical politics contains the seeds of an intellectual renewal. The history of Australian social democracy is different from that of most Western countries because the Hawke-Keating government modernised the country without abandoning the social embeddedness of the market, and the Rudd-Gillard-Rudd government managed the financial crisis without surrendering fiscal rectitude. Based on this experience, Labor can develop once more a vision of government capable of bringing the country together and driving the nation-building reforms needed for a new age of economic prosperity together with a share in the good life.

To do so, the party's main challenge is not only to understand the reasons for losing the 2019 election, but also to learn the lessons of three consecutive defeats – the failure to persuade and win back the working-class vote without which Labor cannot secure a popular or parliamentary majority. Unlike the party's narrow defeat in 2016, the ALP's recent rout comes at a time of greater popular distrust of politics and of public institutions, not least the banks but also systemic corruption in the public sector and the well-documented abuse scandal in the Roman Catholic and other churches. Included in the latter are evangelical Christians – a force in many suburbs and regional areas. They are the faith-based community where Labor's links are weakest. Yet evangelicals are the fastest growing denomination among Christian in Australia. Their energy and interesting vibrancy connect them to hundreds of thousands of Australians. When Rudd was ALP leader, his low-Church Anglicanism connected him to evangelicals, many of whom saw him as a kindred spirit. But since Rudd, there seems no one in Labor at the national level particularly interested in engagement.

Australia finds itself in a paradoxical position of having a more prosperous economy alongside growing precariousness, and greater socio-cultural diversity alongside growing grievances about a lack of social esteem. In this age of upheaval, politics is emphatically not business as usual. To regain the people's trust and win office in 2022, the ALP needs to be bold and exhibit energy. It needs to offer meaning and purpose to a country that superficially is doing well but in reality is sliding into stagnation and failing to confront the forces which threaten its prosperity and security. The country's pressing problems include economic injustice, rapid demographic change, ecological devastation, looming trade wars, and the rise of new foreign powers. Moreover, Labor is vulnerable to seismic forces that have shifted the tectonic plates of the political mainstream in Australia and across the Western world, including the rise of identity politics, a backlash against immigration, the effects of globalisation on shared prosperity, and the impact of technology on the future of work.

Labor has the task of renewing both party and country in ways that might seem irreconcilable. On the one hand, the ALP faces a situation where its centralised institutional power and top-down internal party culture clashes with an increasingly diverse electorate and national community. On the other hand, Labor needs to develop a political platform and policy agenda addressing the needs and interests of working Australians against the backdrop of growing economic and cultural insecurity.

Faced with powerful forces of economic and political polarisation, how should a government hold in balance cultural diversity and social cohesion? The answer is to be found in how the ALP chooses to broker a renewed politics of the common good that reconciles estranged interests – capital and labour, university-educated and vocationally-trained, skilled and unskilled, young and old, Indigenous and immigrant, urban and rural, religious and secular. Beyond binary choices, Labor needs to find ways of sharing power and prosperity with both the disaffected working class and the aspirational middle class.

After building settlements in the 1940s and 1980s, the ALP has the chance to offer a new model. As this book argues, the party's record as a radically reforming government shows that a proper Labor settlement is anchored in a paradoxical politics that blends progressive with conservative principles; it fuses a radical with a traditional character; it combines romantic with rationalist dispositions; it binds together secular with religious values; it embodies a patriotic with an internationalist outlook. Such a paradoxical politics reflects the character of many Australians and suggest that the ALP is the real national party of the people.

Notes

Introduction

[1] Quoted in T. Watts, "The End of the Party? What Labor's History Can Teach Us", *Labor Voice: Journal of Ideas and Discussion*, 9 October 2012, available online at <http://www.laborvoice.com.au/essay/416/>.

[2] N. Dyrenfurth, "'Something old, something new, something borrowed, something blue': the Australian Labor Party" in N. Lawson and A. Pabst (eds), *What's Left? The state of global social democracy* (Labour Together, 2018), p. 37.

[3] B. Shorten, *For the Common Good. Reflections on Australia's Future* (Melbourne University Press, 2016), pp. vii-viii.

[4] N. Dyrenfurth, *A Powerful Influence on Australian Affairs. A new history of the AWU* (Melbourne University Press, 2017).

[5] R. Williams, *In God They Trust? The Religious Beliefs of Australia's Prime Ministers* (Bible Society, 2013).

[6] A. Albanese, transcript of press conference on 25 February 2012: available online at <https://anthonyalbanese.com.au/transcript-of-press-conference>.

[7] B. Fletcher, "Anglicanism and the Shaping of Australian Society", in B. Kaye (ed.), *Anglicanism in Australia* (Melbourne University Press, 2002), p. 308.

[8] *Ibid.*

[9] L. Shilton, "The Way I See It" in *Trade Unions. A Christian View* (Anglican Information Office, 1977), p. 10.

[10] S. Piggin and R. D. Linder, *The Fountain of Public Prosperity: Evangelical Christians in Australian History* 1740–1914 (Monash University Publishing, 2018), p. 468.

[11] A. Atkinson, *The Europeans in Australia: A History* (Oxford University Press, 1997 and 2004), Vol. 1 and 2.

[12] R. Mathews, *Of Labour and Liberty: Distributism in Victoria 1891-1966* (Monash University Publishing, 2017). This seminal book is written by an ALP activist who was the former leader of the Victorian Fabian Society, a minister in Victorian Government, and a federal MP who, as an outsider to Catholicism, came to appreciate Catholic social teaching.

[13] R. Mathews, *Jobs of Our Own: Building a Stakeholder Society: Alternatives to the Market and the State*, 2nd edn (The Distributist Review Press, 2009); on craft unionism, see Dyrenfurth, *A Powerful Influence on Australian Affairs*, ch. 1.

[14] B. Jones, "The capitulation of modern Labor", *The Age*, 22 October 2004.

[15] Proverbs 29:18.

1 Present: The ALP's positioning

[1] D. Marquand, *The Progressive Dilemma: From Lloyd George to Blair*, 2nd edn (Weidenfeld & Nicolson, 1999).

[2] A. Albanese, address to Labor Caucus, 30 May 2019: <https://anthonyalbanese. com.au/address-to-labor-caucus-canberra-thursday-30-may-2019>.

[3] P. Kelly, *Triumph and Demise: The broken promise of a Labor generation* (Melbourne University Press, 2014).

[4] P. Collier, "Denmark has shown how to renew European social democracy", *New Statesman*, 10 June 2019.

[5] J. Chalmers, address to the National Press Club of Australia, 25 June 2019: <https:// www.jimchalmers.org/media/speeches/the-election-the-economy-and-the-46th-parliament/>.

[6] B. Shorten, "The New Centre", *Blue Book*, No. 9 (2004), 889-8810. I am grateful to Nick Dyrenfurth for bringing this document to my attention.

[7] N. Lawson and A. Pabst (eds), *What's Left? The state of global social democracy* (Compass/ Labour Together, 2018).

[8] K. Rudd, *The PM Years* (Macmillan, 2018); W. Swan, *The Good Fight: Six years, two prime ministers and staring down the Great Recession* (Allen & Unwin, 2014).

[9] For an analysis of Bernie Sander's economic programme, see N. Fraser, "From Progressive Neoliberalism to Trump—and Beyond", *American Affairs*, Vol. 1, no. 4 (Winter 2017), pp. 46-64.

[10] D. Brooks, "Do the Democrats Know What Unites Us?", *New York Times*, 5 November 2018.

[11] On progressive patriotism, see the work by T. Soutphommasane, *Reclaiming Patriotism: Nation-Building for Australian Progressives* (Cambridge University Press, 2009) and *The Virtuous Citizen: Patriotism in a Multicultural Society* (Cambridge University Press, 2012).

[12] P. J. Keating, "When the Government Changes, the Country Changes", National Press Club, Canberra, 29 February 1996, quoted in T. Bramston (ed.), *For the True Believers: Great Labor Speeches that Shaped History* (The Federation Press, 2013), p. 104.

[13] Mark Lilla has aptly described identity politics as a form of 'moral panic' in his book, *The Once and Future Liberal. After Identity Politics* (HarperCollins, 2017).

[14] C. Mouffe, *For a Left Populism* (Verso, 2018).

[15] I have argued this in my essay "What the left can learn from Australian Labor", *New Statesman*, 18-24 January 2019, pp. 13-14.

[16] N. Dyrenfurth, "'Something old, something new, something borrowed, something blue': the Australian Labor Party" in N. Lawson and A. Pabst (eds), *What's Left?*, p. 38.

[17] Quoted in Collier.

[18] On the left in the US Democrats, see C. Lasch, *The Agony of the American Left* (Knopf, 1969); *Haven in a Heartless World. The Family Besieged* (Norton, 1977); *The Culture of*

Narcissism. American Life in An Age of Diminishing Expectations (Norton, 1979), as well as Thomas Frank, *Listen, Liberal: Or, What Ever Happened to the Party of the People?* (Scribe, 2016). On the left and the UK Labour Party, see M. Glasman, "The Good Society, Catholic Social Thought and the Politics of the Common Good" in I. Geary and A. Pabst (eds), *Blue Labour: Forging a New Politics*, 2nd edn (I.B. Tauris, 2015), pp. 13-26, and J. Rutherford, 'Conservative Socialism', in *What's Left?*, pp. 95-101. On the French left, see J.-C. Michéa, *Les mystères de la gauche. De l'idéal des Lumières au triomphe du capitalisme absolu* (Edition Climats, 2013) and L. Bouvet, *L'insécurité culturelle. Sortir du malaise identitaire français* (Fayard, 2015).

[19] B. Milanovic, "Global Income Inequality by the Numbers: in History and Now — An Overview—", World Bank Policy Research Working Paper No. 6259 (November 2012): <http://documents.worldbank.org/curated/en/959251468176687085/pdf/wps6259.pdf>.

[20] P. J. Keating, remarks at National Press Club in Canberra on 29 March 2017.

[21] On the new networked generation, see M. Hardt and A. Negri, *Multitude: War and Democracy in the Age of Empire* (Penguin, 2005). For a critique from the perspective of an ethical socialism that is part of the ALP's philosophical traditions, see J. Cruddas, "The humanist left must challenge the rise of cyborg socialism", *The New Statesman*, 20-26 April 2018, pp. 13-14: <https://www.newstatesman.com/politics/uk/2018/04/humanist-left-must-challenge-rise-cyborg-socialism>.

[22] T. Judt, "What Is Living and What Is Dead in Social Democracy?", *New York Review of Books*, 17 December 2009.

[23] J. Kurlantzick, *Democracy in Retreat: The Revolt of the Middle Class and the Worldwide Decline of Representative Government* (Yale University Press, 2013); S. Levitsky and D. Ziblatt, *How Democracies Die* (Viking, 2018); Y. Mounk, *The People vs. Democracy: Why Our Freedom Is in Danger and How to Save It* (Harvard University Press, 2018); D. Runciman, *How Democracy Ends* (Profile Books, 2018). Cf. A. Pabst, *The Demons of Liberal Democracy* (Polity Press, 2019).

[24] For a Marxist critique, see T. Bramble and R. Kuhn, *Labor's Conflict: Big Business, Workers, and the Politics of Class* (Cambridge University Press, 2011). For a liberal critique, see *Fightback!*, the 650-page economic policy package document proposed by John Hewson, the then leader of the Liberal Party ahead of the 1993 election.

[25] J. Wanna, "Australian and New Zealand responses to the 'fiscal tsunami' of the global financial crisis: preparation and precipitous action with the promise of consolidation", in J. Wanna, E. A. Lindquist and J. de Vries (eds), *The Global Financial Crisis and its Budget Impacts in OECD Nations: Fiscal Responses and Future Challenges* (Edward Elgar, 2015), pp. 92-117. For an account by the then Treasurer, see W. Swan, *The Good Fight: Six years, two prime ministers and staring down the Great Recession* (Allen & Unwin, 2014).

[26] A. Mitchell with D. Bassanese, "Economic reform: a barrel of thrills and spills" and R. Willis, "The economy: a perspective from the inside" in S. Ryan and T. Bramston (eds), *The Hawke Government: A Critical Retrospective* (Pluto Press Australia, 2003).

[27] N. Dyrenfurth, "'Something old, something new, something borrowed, something blue': the Australian Labor Party" in *What's Left?*, p. 37.

[28] B. Shorten, address to the National Press Club, 24 August 2016: <http://www.billshorten.com.au/address_to_the_national_press_club_canberra_wednesday_24_august_2016>.

[29] J. Chalmers, "Coalition at the wheel of a ship going nowhere", *The Australian*, 11 June 2019.

[30] Quoted in S. Martin, "'Let's talk about aspiration': Anthony Albanese says Labor must learn from mistakes", *The Guardian*, 30 May 2019.

[31] Albanese, address to Labor Caucus, 30 May 2019.

[32] *Ibid.*

[33] B. Shorten, Opening address of the 48th National Conference of the Australian Labor Party, Adelaide 16 December 2018, p. 6: <https://www.billshorten.com.au/bill_shorten_speech_opening_address_48th_national_conference_of_the_australian_labor_party_adelaide_sunday_16_december_2018>.

[34] Albanese, address to Labor Caucus, 30 May 2019.

[35] See, *supra*, note 5.

[36] *A smart, modern, fair Australia*, ALP National Platform 2016, p. 116: <https://cdn.australianlabor.com.au/documents/ALP_National_Platform.pdf>.

[37] *Ibid.*, p. 117.

[38] *Ibid.*

[39] K. Beazley, "There are dark angels in our nation but there are also good angels", quoted in *For the True Believers*, p. 441.

2 Past: A short history of Labor's ethical purpose

[1] For influential but also problematic accounts, see R. Ward, *The Australian Legend*, 2nd edn (Oxford University Press, 1966); D. Horne, *The Lucky Country* (Penguin, 1964).

[2] Quoted in J. B. Hirst, *Looking for Australia – Historical Essays* (Griffin Press, 2010), p. 147.

[3] *Ibid.*

[4] N. Dyrenfurth, "'Something old, something new, something borrowed, something blue'", in N. Lawson and A. Pabst (eds), *What's Left? The state of global social democracy* (Compass/Labour Together, 2018), p. 38.

[5] C. Hamilton, "Irish-Catholics of New South Wales and the Labor Party, 1890–1910", *Historical Studies: Australia & New Zealand*, Vol. 8, issue 31 (1958), pp. 254-267; A. Connell, "The Bible is not a policy handbook – yet another Christian Australian PM": <https://www.theosthinktank.co.uk/comment/2018/08/28/the-bible-is-not-a-policy-handbook-yet-another-christian-australian-pm>.

[6] B. McKinlay, *The ALP – A Short History of the Australian Labor Party* (Heinemann Publishing, 1981), pp. 1-17.

7   C. Johnson, *The Labor Legacy: Curtin, Chifley, Whitlam, Hawke* (Allen and Unwin, 1989); R. Kuhn, "What a Labor Government Is", *Politics*, Vol. 24 (1989), pp. 147-56; T. Bramble and R. Kuhn, "The transformation of the Australian Labor Party" – Joint Social Sciences Public Lecture, 8 June 2007, Australian National University; T. Bramble and R. Kuhn, *Labor's Conflict: Big Business, Workers, and the Politics of Class* (Cambridge University Press, 2011).

8   B. Nairn, *Civilising Capitalism: The Beginnings of the Australian Labor Party* (Melbourne University Press, 1989).

9   D. Wright, *Alan Walker. Conscience of the Nation* (Open Book Publishers, 1997), pp. 197-8. In 1977 Walker was one of the founders of the Uniting Church of Australia, with most congregations of the Methodist Church of Australasia, about two thirds of the Presbyterian Church of Australia and almost all the churches of the Congregational Union of Australia coming together.

10   T. Kennedy, *Who is Worthy? The Role of Conscience in Restoring Hope to the Church* (Pluto Press, 2000); E. Campion, *Ted Kennedy: Priest of Redfern* (David Lovell Publishing, 2009). I am grateful to Danny Gilbert for conversations about Father Kennedy's legacy.

11   M. Hogan, *Australian Catholics: The Australian Social Justice Tradition* (CollinsDove, 1993); R. Mathews, *Of Labour and Liberty: Distributism in Victoria 1891-1966* (Monash University Publishing, 2017).

12   W. Hudson, *Australian Religious Thought* (Monash University Publishing, 2016), pp. ix-xxiv and 61-92.

13   J. G. Murtagh, *Australia: The Catholic Chapter* (Angus & Robertson, 1959), p. 176.

14   Dyrenfurth, p. 37.

15   Hudson, p. 66.

16   McKinlay, p. 5.

17   C. Lansbury and B. Nairn, "Spence, William Guthrie (1846–1926)", *Australian Dictionary of Biography*, (National Centre of Biography, Melbourne University Press, 1976).

18   Quoted in N. Dyrenfurth and F. Bongiorno, *A Little History of the Australian Labor Party* (University of South Wales Press, 2011), p. 24.

19   F. Bongiorno, *The people's party: Victorian Labor and the Radical Tradition, 1875-1914* (Melbourne University Press, 1996), pp. 11-12.

20   A. Atkinson, *The Europeans in Australia: A History* (Melbourne: Oxford University Press, 1997 and 2004), Vol. 1 and 2.

21   Quoted in B. Stevens and P. Weller, *The Australian Labor Party and Federal Politics: A Documentary Survey* (Melbourne University Press, 1976), p. 72.

22   P. Ford, *Cardinal Moran and the A.L.P. A Study in the Encounter between Moran and Socialism, 1890-1907* (Melbourne University Press, 1966), p. 280.

23   Dyrenfurth and Bongiorno, p. 43.

24   C. M. H. Clark, *A History of Australia. Volume V: The People Make Laws 1888-1915*

(Melbourne University Press, 1981), p. 187.

25 See, for example, C. H. Jory, *The Campion Society and Catholic Social Militancy in Australia, 1929-1939* (Harpham, 1986); T. Ayers, "The National Catholic Rural Movement 1939-1955", BA (Hons.) thesis, University of Melbourne, 1986.

26 T. R. Luscombe, *Builders and Crusaders: Prominent Catholics in Australian History* (Lansdowne Press, 1967).

27 R. Murray, *Labor and Santamaria* (Australian Scholarly Publishing Ltd, 2016), p. 40.

28 Ford, pp. 283-84.

29 P. O'Farrell, *The Catholic Church and Community in Australia: A History* (Thomas Nelson, 1977), p. 303.

30 G. Maddox, *Religion and the Rise of Democracy* (Routledge, 1996).

31 S. Piggin and R. D. Linder, *The Fountain of Public Prosperity: Evangelical Christians in Australian History 1740–1914* (Monash University Publishing, 2018).

32 Hudson, p. xiii. See also S. Piggin, *Spirit of a Nation: The Story of Australia's Christian Heritage* (Strand Publishing, 2004).

33 Quoted in McKinlay, p. 38.

34 Dyrenfurth and Bongiorno, pp. 62-3.

35 *Ibid.*, p. 63.

36 McKinlay, p. 46.

37 W. A. Greening, "The Mannix Thesis in Catholic Secondary Education in Victoria", in E. L. French (ed.), *Melbourne Studies in Education, 1961-62* (Melbourne University Press, 1964), pp. 285-301.

38 Quoted in Dyrenfurth and Bongiorno, p. 69.

39 Murray, pp. 3-4.

40 A. Henderson, *Joseph Lyons: The People's Prime Minister* (NewSouth Publishing, 2011). However, the continued stain of inequality on the fabric of Australian society was criticised, among others, by the *Catholic Worker* and its editor B. A. Santamaria.

41 R. Murray, *The Split: Australian Labor in the Fifties* (Cheshire, 1970); R. Fitzgerald (with the assistance of A. Carr and W. J. Dealey), *The Pope's Battalions: Santamaria, Catholicism and the Labor Split* (University of Queensland Press, 2003).

42 S. Payne, *Fascism in Spain, 1923-1977* (University of Wisconsin Press, 1999), p. 476. See also J. Keene, *Fighting for Franco: International Volunteers in Nationalist Spain During the Spanish Civil War, 1936-39* (Leicester University Press, 2001).

43 K. Treston, "The Australian Reaction to the Spanish Civil War", MA thesis, University of Sydney, 1966.

44 Murray, p. 42.

45 Quoted in G. Henderson, *Santamaria: A Most Unusual Man* (Miegunyah Press, 2015), p. 34.

46 B. A. Santamaria, "We Fight", *Catholic Worker*, No. 1, 1 February, 1936, p. 3.

Quoted in Henderson, *Santamaria*, pp. 134-35.

48 Quoted in *ibid.*, p. 117.

49 Quoted in *ibid.*, pp. 119-120.

50 Australian National Secretariat of Catholic Action: *The Family* (Social Justice Statement 1944), chap. III, point 5, in M. Hogan (ed.), *Justice Now! Social Justice Statements of the Australian Catholic Bishops 1940-1966* (El Faro Press, 1990), p. 59.

51 Quoted in McKinlay, p. 73.

52 Quoted in *ibid.*, pp. 79-80.

53 Dyrenfurth and Bongiorno, p. 96.

54 B. Duncan, *Crusade or Conspiracy? Catholics and the Anti-Communist Struggle in Australia* (University of New South Wales Press, 2001).

55 Quoted in McKinlay, p. 116.

56 Quoted in Henderson, *Santamaria*, pp. 231 and 233.

57 *Ibid.*, p. 235.

58 B.A. Santamaria, *Running the show: selected documents 1939-1996*, ed. by Morgan (Melbourne University Press, 2008), p. 87.

59 P. Strangio, *Neither Power Nor Glory: 100 Years of Political Labor in Victoria, 1856-1956* (Melbourne University Press, 2012).

60 M. Easson, 'Foreword' to S. Short, *Laurie Short. A Political Life* (Allen & Unwin in association with the Lloyd Ross Forum, 1992), p. xi.

61 J. Zubrzycki, *Arthur Calwell and the Origin of Post-War Immigration* (AGPS, 1995), pp. 4-5.

62 Calwell, "What the Popes Have Said on Capitalism, the Employing Class and Trade Unions": <http://digital.slv.vic.gov.au/view/action/singleViewer.do?dvs=1556404724757~362&locale=en_US&metadata_object_ratio=10&show_metadata=true&VIEWER_URL=/view/action/singleViewer.do?&preferred_usage_type=VIEW_MAIN&DELIVERY_RULE_ID=10&frameId=1&usePid1=true&usePid2=true>.

63 *Ibid.*

64 Quoted in McKinlay, p. 138.

65 Dyrenfurth and Bongiorno, pp. 126-7.

3 Philosophy: Labor's traditions and dispositions

1 L. Wittgenstein, *Philosophical Investigations*, ed. with a revised translation by G. E. M. Anscombe (Macmillan, 1953), p. 32.

2 See N. Timothy, "The crisis of conservatism", *The New Statesman*, 20 June 2018. On conservatism in Australia, see D. Freeman, *Abbott's Right: The Conservative Tradition from Menzies to Abbott* (Melbourne University Press, 2017).

3 T. Judt, *Ill Fares the Land: A Treatise On Our Present Discontents* (Penguin, 2011).

4 A. Métin, *Le socialisme sans doctrines: la question agraire et la question ouvrière en Australie et*

Nouvelle-Zélande (Alcan, 1901); English translation: *Socialism Without Doctrine*, transl. R. Ward (Alternative Publishing Cooperative, 1977).

5   N. Dyrenfurth, "It's the culture, stupid" in N. Dyrenfurth and T. Soutphommasane (eds), *All That's Left: What Labor Should Stand For* (University of New South Wales Press, 2010), pp. 15-35, quote at p. 18.

6   See A. Henderson, *Federation's Man of Letters: Patrick McMahon Glynn* (Kapunda Press, 2019).

7   L. Ross, "The Philosophy of the Australian Labor Party", *The Antioch Review*, Vol. 7, no. 1 (Spring, 1947), pp. 109-124, quote at p. 112. On Ross, see M. Hearn, "Means and Ends: The Ideology of Dr. Lloyd Ross", *Labour History*, No. 63 (November 1992), pp. 25-42.

8   N. Dyrenfurth, *Mateship: A Very Australian History* (Scribe, 2015).

9   Quoted in Ross, p. 114.

10   Quoted in *ibid.*, p. 116.

11   For a critique of labourism, see V. Burgmann, *In Our Time: Socialism and the Rise of Labor 1885-1905* (Allen & Unwin, 1985); cf. R. Markey, *The Making of the Labor Party in New South Wales 1880-1900* (New South Wales University Press, 1988). A corrective can be found in N. Dyrenfurth, *Heroes & Villains. The rise and fall of the early Australian Labor Party* (Australian Scholarly Publishing, 2011).

12   T. Battin, "A break from the past: The labor party and the political economy of Keynesian social democracy", *Australian Journal of Political Science*, Vol. 28, no. 2 (1993), pp. 221-41; T. Battin, "Keynesianism, Socialism, and Labourism, and the Role of Ideas in Labor Ideology", *Labour History*, No. 66 (1994), pp. 33-44.

13   T. H. Irving, "Socialism, Working Class Mobilisation, and the Origins of the Labor Party" in B. O'Meagher (ed.), *The Socialist Objective: Labor and Socialism* (Hale and Iremonger, 1983).

14   C. Johnson, *The Labor Legacy: Curtin, Chifley, Whitlam, Hawke* (Allen & Unwin, 1989); R. Kuhn, "What a Labor Government Is", *Politics*, Vol. 24 (1989), pp. 147-56; B. Frankel, "Beyond Labourism and Socialism: How the Australian Labor Party Developed the Model of 'New Labour'", *New Left Review*, 1/221 (Jan.-Feb. 1997), pp. 1-33; T. Bramble and R. Kuhn, "Continuity or Discontinuity in the Recent History of the Australian Labor Party?", *Australian Journal of Political Science*, Vol. 44, no. 2 (2009), pp. 281-94; T. Bramble and R. Kuhn, *Labor's Conflict: Big Business, Workers, and the Politics of Class* (Cambridge University Press, 2011).

15   H. McQueen, "Labourism and Socialism" in R. Gordon (ed.), *The Australian New Left: Critical Essays and Strategy* (Heinemann Australia, 1970), p. 59.

16   G. Maddox, *The Hawke Government and Labor Tradition* (Penguin, 1989).

17   G. Maddox and T. Battin, "Australian Labor and the Socialist Tradition", *Australian Journal of Political Science*, Vol. 26, no. 2 (1991), pp. 181-96, quote at p. 195.

18   B. Jones, "Gough Whitlam's vision of social democracy: Parliament and party", Whitlam Institute, 2016.

19   "Bob Hawke mourns his father's death", *The Canberra Times*, 24 December 1989, p. 3.

20   B. Hawke, *The Hawke Memoirs* (Heinemann, 1994), p. 137.

21   Australian Catholic Council for Employment Relations (ACCER), "The Harvester minimum wage case and its importance to Australian society after 110 years", extract from the ACCER submission to the Annual Wage Review 2016-17 conducted by the Fair Work Commission in Sydney on 18 May 2017: <http://www.accer.asn.au/index.php/papers/146-the-harvester-minimum-wage-case-and-its-importance-to-australian-society-after-110-years/file>.

22   J.A. Ryan, "Bernhard Ringrose Wise", *Journal of the Royal Historical Society*, Vol. 81, Part 1 (June 1995), pp. 71-84.

23   G. Melleuish, *Cultural Liberalism in Australia: A study in intellectual and cultural history* (Cambridge University Press, 1995); G. Melleuish, *A Short History of Australian Liberalism* (Centre for Independent Studies, 2001).

24   A. Leigh MP, "Social liberalism fits Labor", *The Saturday Paper*, 29 June – 5 July 2019.

25   C. Berg, "Adam Smith and Jeremy Bentham in the Australian colonies", *History of Economics Review*, Vol. 68, no. 1 (2017), pp. 2-16.

26   H. Collins, "Political Ideology in Australia: The Distinctiveness of a Benthamite Society", *Daedalus*, Vol. 114, no. 1 (1985), pp. 147-69.

27   G. Melleuish and S. A. Chavura, "Utilitarianism Contra Sectarianism: The Official and Unauthorised Civic Religion of Australia" in W. O. Coleman (ed.), *Only in Australia: The History, Politics, and Economics of Australian Exceptionalism* (Oxford University Press, 2016), pp. 62-80. I find many of the ideas here by Melleuish and Chavura illuminating and suggestive rather than conclusively clinched – the idea of profoundly religious utilitarianism being one such instance.

28   Berg, p. 11.

29   M. Easson, "What It Means to be Labor" in M. Easson (ed.), *The Foundations of Labor* (Pluto Press in Association with the Lloyd Ross Forum of the Labor Council of NSW, 1990), pp. 71-80, quote at p. 77.

30   B. Nairn, *Civilising Capitalism: The Beginnings of the Australian Labor Party* (Melbourne University Press, 1989).

31   Easson, 'What It Means to be Labor', p. 77.

32   S. MacIntyre, "Who are the True Believers?", *Labour History*, Vol. 68 (May 1995), p. 158.

33   G. Maddox, "Revisiting Tradition: Labor and Socialism", *Overland*, no. 173 (2003), pp. 56-7.

34   D. Furse-Roberts, "Burke's Legacy in Australian Politics", *Quadrant*, Vol. LXII, Number 7-8, No. 548 (July 2018).

35   M. Easson, "The Liberalism of Richard Bourke", *Quadrant*, Vol. 62, no. 11, (November 2018), pp. 54-58.

36   I. Kramnick, "The Left and Edmund Burke", *Political Theory*, Vol. 11, no. 2 (May 1983), pp. 189-214, quote at p. 200.

37   I argue this in greater detail in my book with John Milbank, *The Politics of Virtue: Post-liberalism and the Human Future* (Rowman & Littlefield International, 2016), pp. 13-67.

38   J. Dickenson, *Renegades and Rats. Betrayal and the Remaking of Radical Organisations in Britain and Australia* (Melbourne University Press, 2006), p. 27.

39   A. A. Calwell, *Labor's Role in Modern Society* (Cheshire-Lansdowne, 1965), pp. 39-40.

40   A. A. Calwell, *Be Just and Fear Not* (Lloyd O'Neil, 1972), p. 243.

41   B. Jones, maiden speech, 12 September 1972: <https://www.parliament.vic.gov.au/images/stories/historical_hansard/VicHansard_19720905_19720913.pdf, pp. 197, 200-1>.

42   B. Jones, *Hansard*, House of Representatives, 22 March 1979. As Michael Easson has shown, other Labor MPs have cited those same words by Burke, including Nick Champion, Member for Wakefield, *Hansard*, House of Representatives, 10 September 2012 and Michael Danby, Member for Melbourne Ports, *Hansard*, House of Representatives, 2 April 2019.

43   B. Jones, "Relevance of the French Revolution in 2016", in *Knowledge. Courage. Leadership* (Wilkinson Publishing, 2016), p. 241.

44   R. B. Scotton and C. R. Macdonald, *The Making of Medibank* (School of Health Services Management, University of New South Wales, 1993).

45   M. Easson, *Keating's and Kelty's Super Legacy: The Birth and Relentless Threats to the Australian System of Superannuation*, (Connor Court, 2017), p. 213.

46   M. Easson, "A Sterile Debate", *Australian Left Review*, Issue 140 (June 1992), pp. 30-31.

47   M. Easson, "Edmund Burke and Australian Labor" in D. Freeman (ed.), *The Market's Morals: Responding to Jesse Norman* (Kapunda Press, 2019), *forthcoming*.

48   W. Hudson, *Australian Religious Thought* (Monash University Publishing, 2016), p. xi.

49   S. Piggin and R. D. Linder, *The Fountain of Public Prosperity: Evangelical Christians in Australian History 1740–1914* (Monash University Publishing, 2018).

50   H. Lawson, "The New Religion" in *A Camp-Fire Yarn: Henry Lawson Complete Works 1885-1900*, ed. L. Cronin (Lansdowne Press, 1984), p. 112.

51   Hudson, pp. 61-81 and P. Hempenstall, *The Meddlesome Priest. A Life of Ernest Burgmann* (Allen & Unwin, 1993).

52   A number of influential groups and journals promoted Catholic social teaching and cognate ideas, including the Campion Society, *The Catholic Worker*, *Twentieth Century*, and *Morpeth Review* – the latter being a quarterly of largely Anglo-Catholic persuasion, inspired by Burgmann and others associated with St John's at Morpeth, near Newcastle in NSW. See, among other examples, L. Ross, "Socialism and Distributivism", *Twentieth Century*, Vol.1, no. 4 (June 1947), pp. 32-47 and *idem.*, "Labour, Catholicism, and Democratic Socialism", *Twentieth Century*, Vol. 2, no. 2 (December 1947), pp. 74-89. For a concise yet comprehensive account of how Christian social teaching shaped the ALP and Australian politics more widely, see Hudson, *Australian Religious Thought*, pp. xx-xix, 82-92.

53   R. J. L. Hawke, The Inaugural Bishop Manning Lecture, Thursday 7th October 2010, Sydney.

54   K. Blackburn, "The Living Wage in Australia: A Secularization of Catholic Ethics on Wages, 1891–1907", *Journal of Religious History*, Vol. 20, no. 1 (June 1996), pp. 93-113; M. Sawer, *The Ethical State? Social Liberalism in Australia* (Melbourne University Press, 2003). Cf. J. Murphy, *A Decent Provision. Australian Welfare Policy, 1870 to 1949* (Ashgate, 2011).

55   *Hansard*, Debates of the Australasian Federal Convention, Third session, Melbourne, 22 January – 17 March 1898.

56   Hawke, The Inaugural Bishop Manning Lecture.

57   "Harvester Case of 1907", pp. 3-4: <https://www.aph.gov.au/binaries/library/intguide/law/harvester.pdf>.

58   Hawke says in his Inaugural Bishop Manning Lecture that one of the Judges of the Court, Alfred 'Alf' Foster, a former Labor activist and a member of the Commonwealth Arbitration Court from 1944 to his death in 1962, told him in 1959 that the President of the Court in 1953, The Hon. Raymond Kelly, a devout Catholic and sympathiser of Santamaria's views, was lobbied by Santamaria in 1953 on what the Court should determine. This is interesting hearsay that merits further investigation.

59   Hawke, The Inaugural Bishop Manning Lecture.

60   P. J. Keating, "Traditions of Labor in Power; Whitlam and Hawke in the Continuum" in S. Loosley (ed.), *Traditions for Reform in New South Wales. Labor History Essays* (Pluto Press, 1987), p. 186.

61   W. Lane, in *The Worker*, quoted in Burgmann, *In Our Time*, p. 71.

62   J. Gillard MP, speech at the National Press Club, 17 September 2008.

63   T. Soutphommasane, "Social Justice and the Good Society" in N. Dyrenfurth and T. Soutphommasane (eds), *All That's Left. What Labor Should Stand For* (University of New South Wales Press, 2010), pp. 37-56.

64   For this quote and some of the ideas in this section, I am indebted to conversations with Jonathan Rutherford and his as yet unpublished work.

65   Collins, *op. cit.*; Berg, *op. cit.*

66   M. Lilla, *The Once and Future Liberal. After Identity Politics* (HarperCollins, 2017).

67   C. Lasch, *The Revolt of the Elites and the Betrayal of Democracy* (Norton, 1995).

68   D. Miller, *Strangers in Our Midst: The Political Philosophy of Immigration* (Harvard University Press, 2016).

69   J. Gray, *Heresies: Against Progress and Other Illusions* (Granta, 2004); J, Gray, *The Silence of Animals: On Progress and Other Modern Myths* (Farrar, Straus & Giroux, 2013).

4 Politics and Policy Renewing party and country

[1] A. Albanese, address to Labor Caucus, 30 May 2019: <https://anthonyalbanese.com.au/address-to-labor-caucus-canberra-thursday-30-may-2019>.

[2] T. Judt, "What Is Living and What Is Dead in Social Democracy?", *New York Review of Books*, 17 December 2009.

[3] C. H. Achen and L. M. Bartels, *Democracy for Realists: Why Elections Do Not Produce Responsive Government* (Princeton University Press, 2016), p. 319. See also G. L. Cohen, "Party Over Policy: The Dominating Impact of Group Influence on Political Beliefs", *Journal of Personality and Social Psychology*, Vol. 85, no. 5 (2003), pp. 808–822.

[4] On how community organising can help to renew social democracy, see A. Graf, "Community Organising and Blue Labour" in I. Geary and A. Pabst (eds), *Blue Labour: Forging a New Politics*, 2nd edn (I.B. Tauris, 2015), pp. 71-78.

[5] T. Bentley, "The ALP: strategy, narrative and party organisation" in *What's Left? The state of global social democracy* (Compass/Labour Together, 2018), pp. 29-34.

[6] Graf, pp. 71-73.

[7] For an inside account of the Blair/Brown party machine, see P. Gould, *The Unfinished Revolution: How New Labour Changed British Politics Forever* (Abacus, 2011); for a critique of how New Labour lost five million voters, mostly working class supporters, and how it was defeated everywhere by everyone in the 2015 general election which the then leader Ed Miliband was confident of winning, see J. Cruddas, N. Pecorelli and J. Rutherford, *Labour's Future: Why Labour lost in 2015 and how it can win again* (Labour Together, 2016).

[8] Bentley, p. 32.

[9] N. Dyrenfurth, "Labor's Right Mess", *The Saturday Paper*, 18 April 2015.

[10] Bentley, p. 32.

[11] P. J. Keating, "Voluntary euthanasia is a threshold moment for Australia, and one we should not cross", *The Sydney Morning Herald*, 19 October 2017.

[12] A. West, "How religious voters lost faith in Labor: Lessons from the 2019 federal election", ABC Religion & Ethics, 24 May 2019: < https://www.abc.net.au/religion/how-religious-voters-lost-faith-in-labor/11146850> (original italics).

[13] *Ibid.*

[14] P. Dodson, speech in the Australian Senate, 15 August 2018.

[15] *Ibid.*

[16] *Ibid.*

[17] Mentioned in the first social encyclical *Rerum Novarum* of 1891, the idea of the "living wage" was subsequently developed by the Catholic priest John A. Ryan in his eponymous book, *A Living Wage: Its Ethical and Economic Aspects* (Macmillan, 1914).

[18] H. Cottam, *Radical Help: How We Can Remake the Relationships Between Us and Revolutionise the Welfare State* (Virage, 2018).

[19] R. Mathews, *Jobs of Our Own: Building a Stakeholder Society: Alternatives to the Market and the State*, 2nd edn (The Distributist Review Press, 2009).

[20] J. Chalmers and M. Quigley, *Changing Jobs: The Fair Go in the New Machine Age* (Redback

Quarterly, 2017).

[21] Geary and Pabst, *Blue Labour.*

[22] M. Glasman, "A Vocational Economy" in *Common Good Economics* (forthcoming).

[23] A. MacIntyre, *After Virtue. A study in moral theory* (Duckworth, 1981), p. 191.

[24] M. Elam, "Markets, Morals and the Powers of Innovation", *Economy and Society*, Vol. 22, no. 1 (1993), pp. 1-41.

[25] S. Turner, *The Social Theory of Practices: tradition, tacit knowledge and presuppositions* (University of Chicago Press, 1994); W. Streeck, "Beneficial Constraints: on the economic limits of rational voluntarism" in J. R. Hollingsworth and R. Boyer (eds), *Contemporary Capitalism: The Embeddedness of Institutions* (Cambridge University Press, 1997), pp. 197-219.

[26] N. Dyrenfurth, "TAFE should no longer be the poor cousin to university", *The Sydney Morning Herald*, 27 January 2019.

[27] T. Piketty, *Le capital au XXIe siècle* (Seuil, 2013).

[28] M. Young, *The Rise of the Meritocracy* (Thames and Hudson, 1958); M. Young, "Down with Meritocracy", *The Guardian*, 29 June 2001.

[29] Piketty, p. 662.

[30] D. Miller, *Strangers in Our Midst: The Political Philosophy of Immigration* (Harvard University Press, 2016).

[31] P. J. Keating, "Redfern Speech (Year for the World's Indigenous People)", delivered in Redfern Park on 10 December 1992: <https://antar.org.au/sites/default/files/paul_keating_speech_transcript.pdf>.

[32] K. Rudd, motion moved on Apology to the Indigenous Australian 'Stolen Generation', *Hansard*, 13 February 2008.

[33] Uphold & Recognise, *A Fuller Declaration of Australia's Nationhood: Options for Discussion*: see <www.upholdandrecognise.com>.

[34] *Ibid.*, p. 8.

[35] M. J. Sandel, "The procedural republic and the unencumbered self", *Political Theory*, Vol. 12, no. 1 (1984), pp. 81-96, quote at p. 94.

[36] K. Beazley, in conversation with the Strategist Six: see < https://www.aspistrategist.org.au/the-strategist-six-kim-beazley-2/>.

Conclusion The purpose of power

[1] G. Freudenberg, *Cause for Power – The Official History Of The New South Wales Branch of The Australian Labor Party* (Pluto Press, 1991), p. 34.

[2] B. Nairn, *Civilising Capitalism: The Beginnings of the Australian Labor Party* (Melbourne University Press, 1989).

[3] M. Sandel, "The energy of the Brexiteers and Trump is born of the failure of elites", interview with Jason Cowley, *New Statesman*, 13 June 2016.

[4] *Ibid.*

Index

www.ingramcontent.com/pod-product-compliance
Lightning Source LLC
Chambersburg PA
CBHW050353270326
41926CB00016B/3722